# THIS IS MY GENERATION

## Rock legends of the 1950s, 60s, 70s, and 80s on stage today

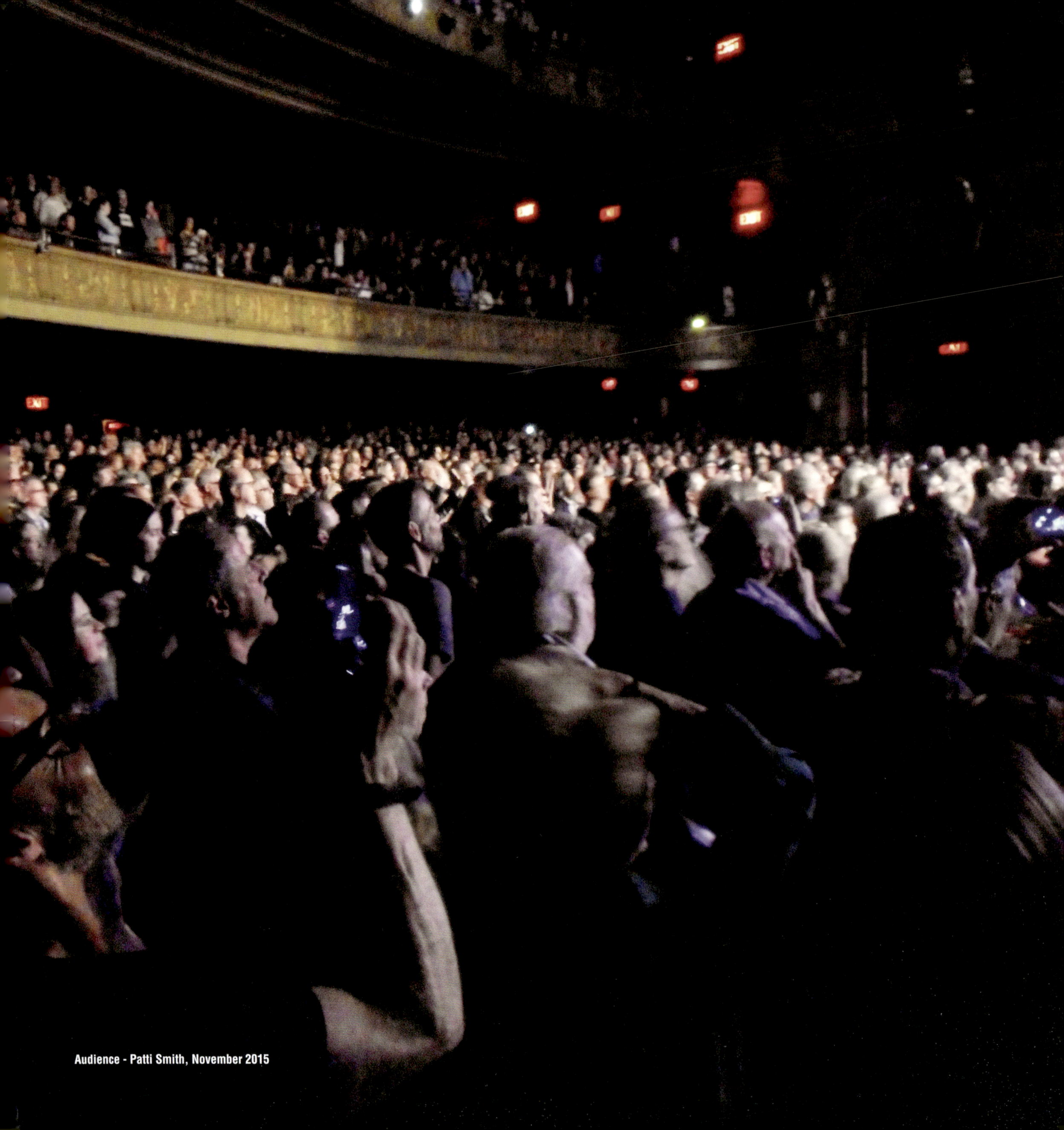

Audience - Patti Smith, November 2015

# *Introduction*

**by Bob Eisenberg**

From my perch precariously cantilevered beyond the vaguely reassuring tree-trunk of incipient Geezerdom I am forced to ask myself the most disquieting of questions regardless of the subject:  What happened?

But in this instance I refer in particular to the demise of the rock star replete with boundless adulation of the unsung millions, a phenomenon emanating from the seedling of organic community spontaneously and simultaneously eagerly concurring on the metaphysical singularity of a sentient musical phenomenon only to be replaced by the eminently forgettable coddled corporate avatars with fetid evanescence wafting in a breeze, whose names are sooner consigned to the void than a random episode of a particularly bad sitcom.  All pizazz and no substance would make me despondent to the point of apathy but the music to which we passionately adhere rescues us from oblivion.

Not only has popular music been driven off a cliff and into a canyon of mediocrity, even background elevator music has been meticulously sanitized of any stray remnants of passion evoked by musicianship that had its heyday in the 1960s but continues to this day like the ever-thinning tail of a particularly agile mouse. Innocuous 50s muzak floods the aisles of made-in-China bric-a-brac constituting anonymous Big Box emporiums. Which is probably all for the best, as the authentic passion on display in this book of extraordinary photography dare not be besmirched by the quotidian duplicity of soulless corporate behemoth-like factories.

And wither these stars? Wither the stories of legendary excess and tales of superhuman bursts of lyrical creativity giving way to the varied sounds and compelling hooks engraved upon our souls to this day--that is, if we are of a certain age and/or inclination.

The sheer energy released by these musicians and conveyed uninterrupted by any banal reaches of commerce to the listener which in turn bestows energy on the listener--that energy, like a fading heavenly entity is still with us, but in seemingly calibrated lower doses. As for the future, whether the music made by these emblematic artists of the earth-shattering genre commonly referred to as rock'n'roll fades into the distance and becomes ossified like some set-in-stone oeuvre to be "appreciated" by generations henceforth like the classical works of Old Europe, or whether it will be revivified with an as yet unparalleled vigor remains to be seen. But as for now, the music evokes an energy and visceral satisfaction almost as powerfully as ever--almost.

We're not dead yet--and with songs by the likes of the Stones or Crosby, Stills, Nash and Young we never will be. Long after Rihanna becomes the answer to a Final Jeopardy question which none of the contestants answers correctly, that couch on the cover of the CSN album, with its tattered edges and untamable stuffing, will be remembered down to the last button, just as Suite: Judy Blue Eyes will be lovingly recollected to the abrupt final a capella note.

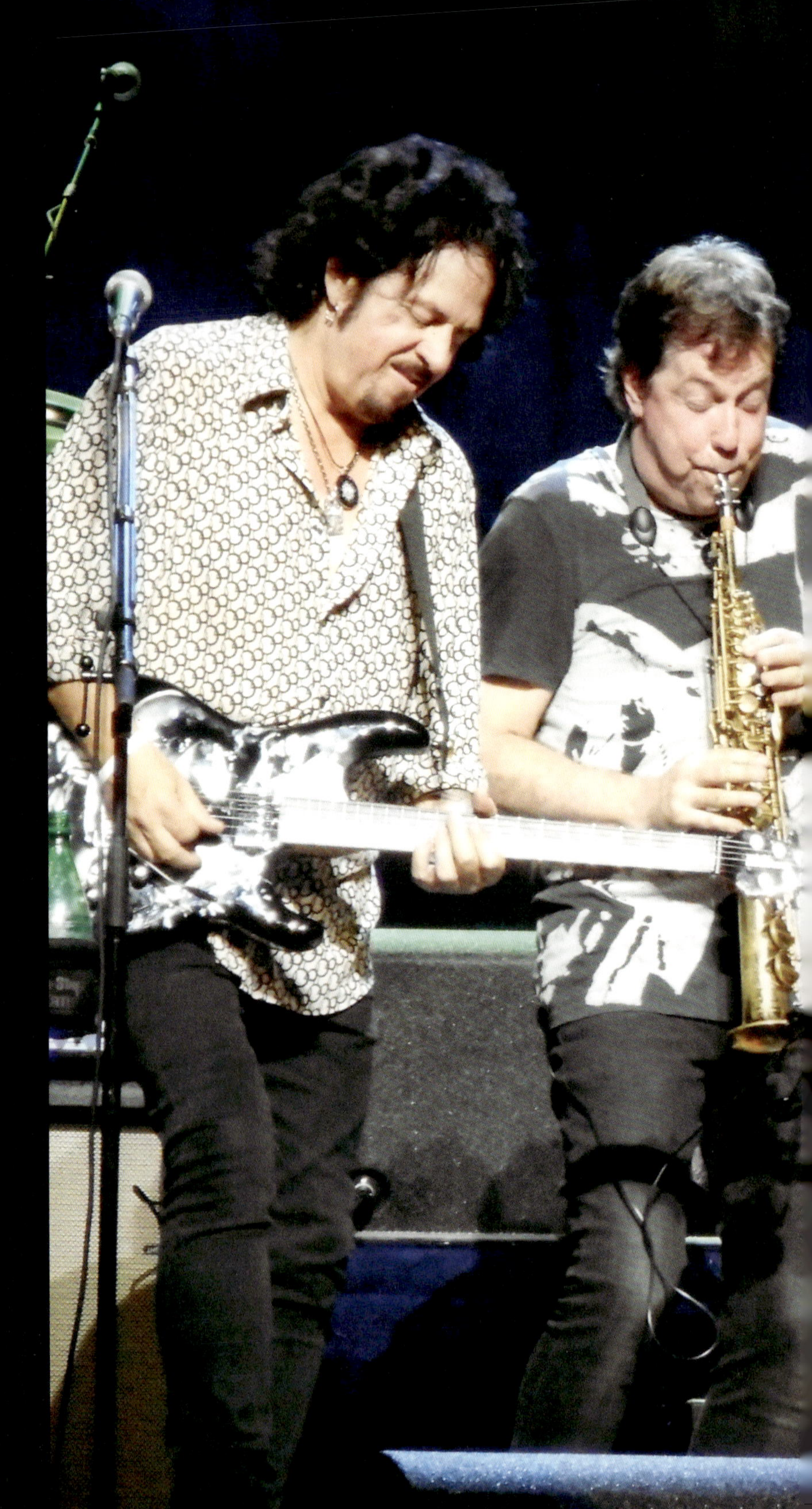

Ringo's All-Starr Band, from right:
Ringo Starr (Beatles)
Richard Page (Mr. Mister)
Todd Rundgren (Utopia)
Warren Ham
Steve Lukather (Toto)
June 2014

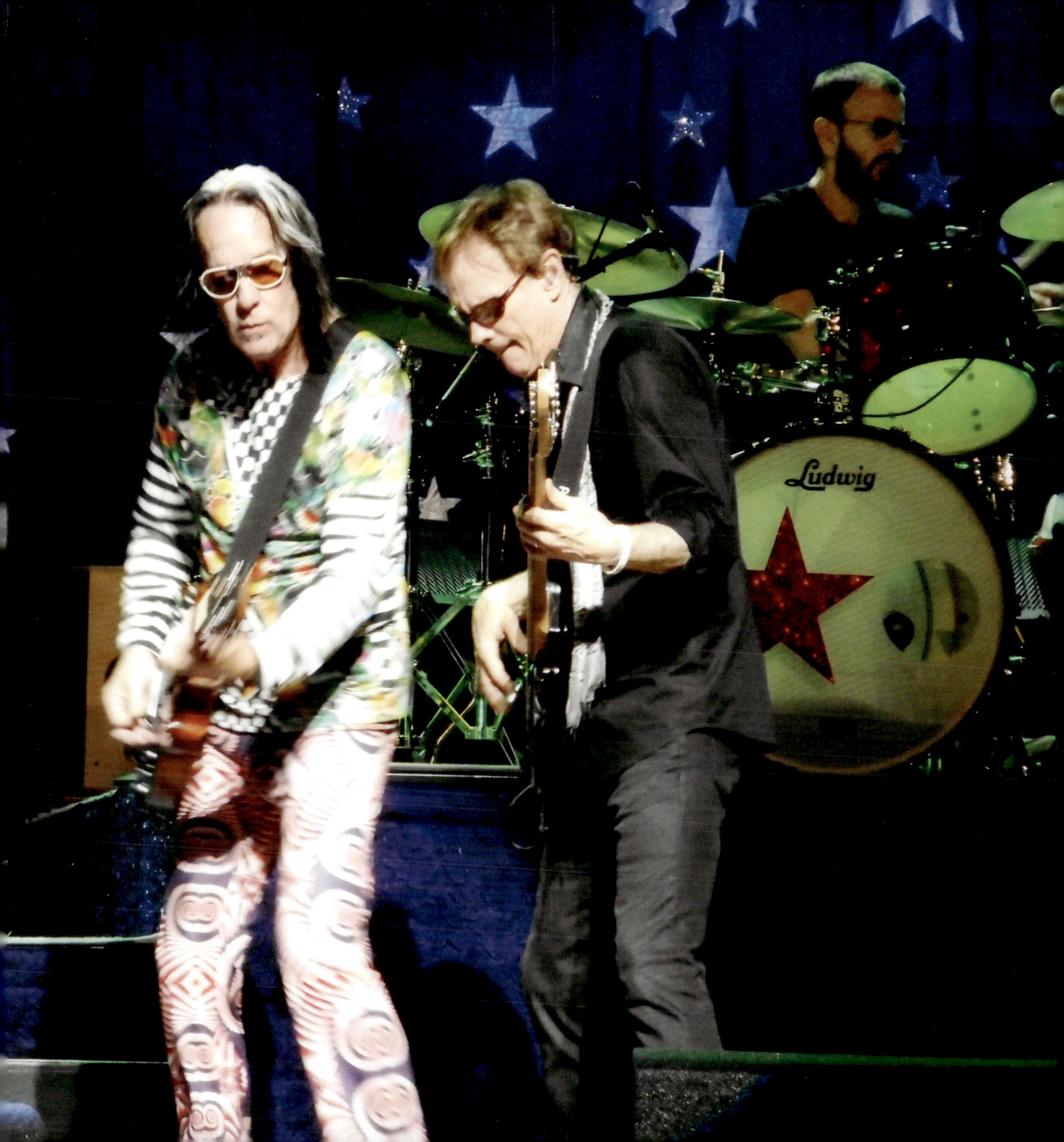

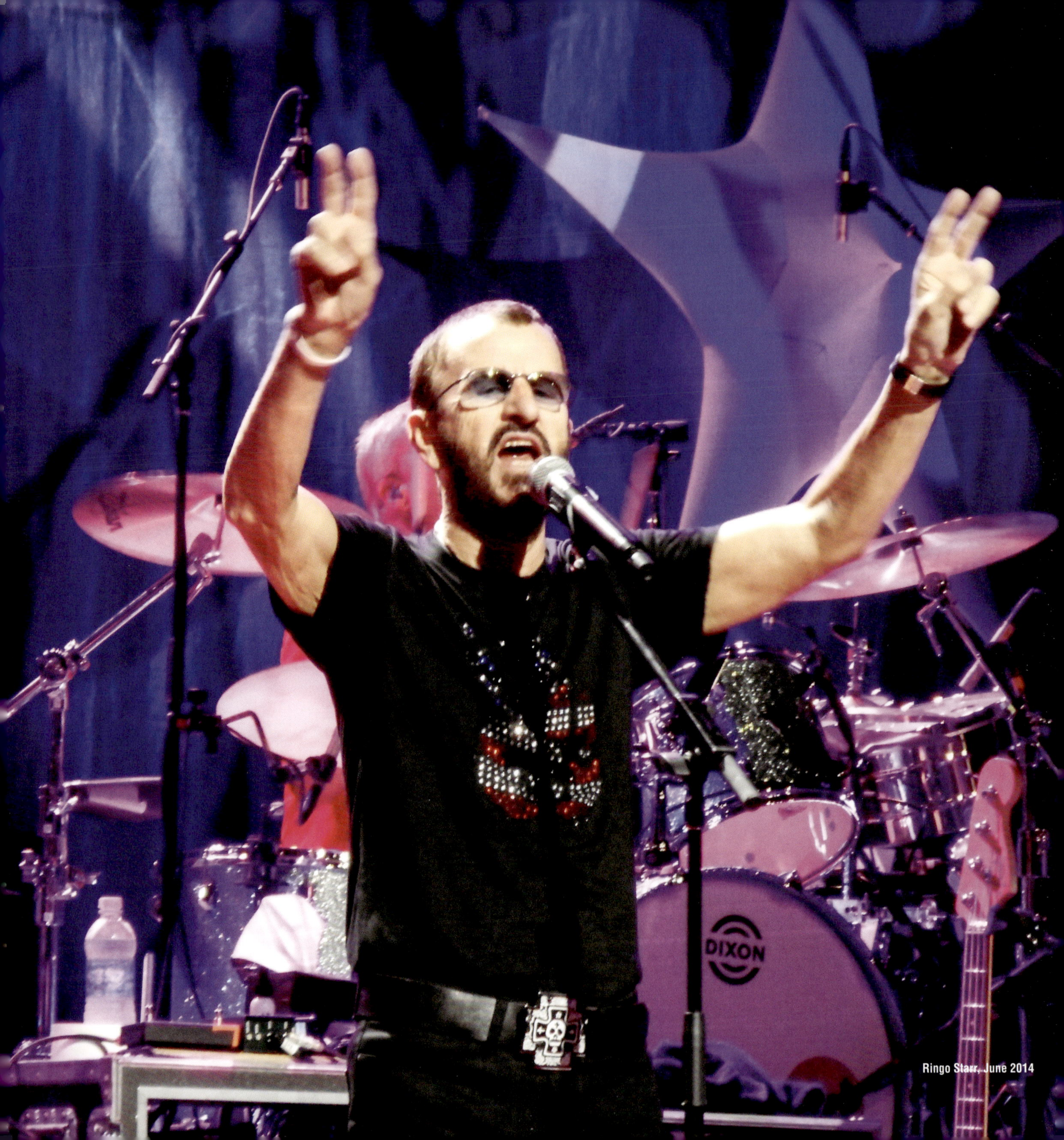



Ringo Starr, June 2014

# This Is My Generation

*by Roger Harris*

**Rock legends of the 1950s, 60s, 70s, and 80s - on stage today.**

Robby Krieger, the song-writer and guitarist for The Doors, plays classic hit after hit (including Light My Fire which he wrote) with his current band. Robby is 70 years old and rocks the house like a typhoon. His unique virtuoso style has earned him a place in the Rock and Roll Hall of Fame, and a position on every list of the greatest rock guitarists of all time. After tearing it up on ''Love Me Two Times'', Robby steps up to the mic. A respectful hush falls over the awestruck crowd.

"I wrote that song during the Vietnam War".
What? Wait a minute, what are the lyrics? "Love me two times, I'm going away." Going away... and probably never coming back. Ooo. Stomach punch.

I was originally going to call this book, "Guys From the 60s in their seventies, and Guys from the 70s in their sixties. Plus a few guys from the 50s in their eighties and a few guys from the 80s in their fifties". But that was a tad too long. Of course if I had written it ten years ago I could have called it, "Guys from the 60s in their sixties".

Rock music started as a fad. Like the hula hoop or the twist. Everybody's doing it for the summer, but by next fall nobody even remembers it. If you're going to make a movie about it, you'd better make it quick, because by the time the film gets to the theaters the fad might be over. And who cares about last month's fad? The squares.

Sha Na Na said it best: "I don't care what people say, rock and roll is here to stay". So what were people saying? They were saying that rock and roll was a fad. Gone like flag-pole sitting. Or it will be gone. Soon. After the summer. Next winter for sure. But here we are 50 years later and we are bigger than ever! Rock music changed the music industry, changed the generation, changed the world. We ended the war.

You can hike through the jungles of Peru, climb to the top of Machu Picchu, and there will be someone wearing a Ramones t-shirt. I've seen this with my own eyes. We are ubiquitous.

Opera is awesome, theater is terrific, ballet is beautiful, but there is nothing like a rock concert. Seeing your favorite singers, song-writers, and musicians play your favorite songs. What could be finer? A great rock concert is not just a show, it's an event. Woodstock was not a rock concert. It was history. A great show can change you. It can change the world. Or it can simply be great fun. For me, seeing Paul McCartney play songs that I remember listening to as a child brought tears to my eyes. Seeing Mick Jagger on stage so clearly enjoying his work, seeing Keith Moon going absolutely insane on stage... it changed me. I spent over twenty years of my life as a performing artist inspired by the works of our rock and roll brothers and sisters.

I will never forget, at age 4, the time my 11-year-old sister burst through the door and started screaming, ''the Beatles have a new song that goes 'yeah yeah yeah'! Eeeeeeeeee!" The time: April 1964; the song: She Loves You.

What happened to the great artists of the 60s and 70s? What happened to that fad called Rock and Roll? Some of them are still on stage. And have they lost that star quality that made us jump and dance? No, they haven't. And I have the pictures to prove it. So here are a couple of years of recent rock, blues, and pop concerts, mostly in New York, 2013 to 2016.

When the performer is on his mark and the music hits you it's profoundly moving. There's something about seeing Paul up close, in person that is unlike anything else. The man invented the 60s, defined the era. The man shaped rock music. Which leads to the question that has been asked a thousand times, what made the Beatles the best? And of course, 'who was greater, John or Paul?' And, 'who's your favorite Beatle?'

For one thing, the Beatles had everything. They were all cute. Incredibly cute. That helped. They wrote the best tunes and had thought-provoking lyrics. Funny lyrics, romantic lyrics, profound lyrics, silly lyrics. But always entertaining. They were sometimes fun, sometimes serious, and sometimes sentimental. Sometimes controversial. But they were ALL these things. So they were universal. They had something for everyone. They had a range. They were also superb musicians and had excellent voices. That helped.

But the main thing was the John/Paul dynamic that kept the group ever on edge. John's songs and voice dig into your guts. John is like a slow drill entering your body and sticking to your viscera. John is always striving, always searching. Never quite there, always reaching for the unattainable. Reaching for love. "I should have known better". Reaching for meaning. "How does it feel to be one of the beautiful people?" Reaching for enlightenment, "Turn off your mind, relax and float downstream."

Paul, contra-distinctly, wasn't reaching for anything. He was there. "I saw her standing there". "I love you, I love you, I love you, my Michelle". That's all there is to it. John is the 'potential energy', and Paul is the 'kinetic energy'. John is, "I do all the pleasing with you, it's so hard to reason with you". Paul is, "a love like ours will never die". And the constant contrast between the two, the competition, the juxtaposition, it made the band dynamic like no other. Two opposites, extremes, a million light years apart, yet as close as two sides of the same coin.

And when they were together, John always just a hair ahead, always the leader, always keeping Paul from completely taking off and flying away. And Paul keeping John on his toes, forcing him to push harder and harder. There has never been a set of albums like the Beatles. One after another. Each one achieving the impossible feat of out-doing the one before. How can you top 'Meet the Beatles' with "I Wanna Hold Your Hand', 'I Saw Her Standing There', and 'Not A Second Time'? Then, when all eyes in the civilized world were on them, they come out with "She Loves You, yeah yeah yeah," to blow everyone's mind. The Beatles had five songs in the top ten at the same time. It doesn't even make sense.

Then "Rubber Soul". How can you beat that? Then "Revolver". Okay you beat that but you'll never do it again. Then "Sgt. Pepper", arguably the greatest single work of creative artistic expression of the century. Then "Magical Mystery Tour" (my personal fave), "White Album" (more correctly titled 'the Beatles'), then "Let It Be" then "Abbey Road". They were a ticking time bomb of creativity that finally exploded. (Most of the album "Let it Be" was recorded before "Abbey Road", though it was released after.) Many consider "Abbey Road" to be their best work.

And then John was all on his own without Paul to keep him on edge and his music suffered. His political activism didn't suffer, but his music did. But Paul was also on his own and he flourished. John created several iconic anthems in, for example "Give Peace a Chance" and "Imagine". But Paul was producing one hit after another for years. Because John is the potential energy. "Give Peace a Chance." Always striving for the unattainable. But Paul is the kinetic energy, "Some people want to fill the world with silly love songs. What's wrong with that?" John is saying 'give peace a chance' but Paul is actually giving peace a chance. He is being peace. He is being love. He's not striving for it, he is it. And of course being it is never as interesting as hoping for it. The cold soda on a hot day is never as great as you expect it to be when you're thirsty. When you finally get to Paris, it's awesome, it's lovely, it's the best. But it's still you worrying about money and feeling a little nauseous. It's Paris, not heaven. That's what we're fighting for? Singing silly love songs? That's what we're protesting for, getting shot in Ohio, giving our lives? Singing silly love songs? Well, yes, actually it is.

So who's my favorite Beatle? John, while the Beatles are together, Paul after they each go solo. Musically, not necessarily as people. That's my story and I'm sticking to it.

Before we talk about the Grateful Dead, let's talk about the origins of rock music and the British invasion. But who really invented Rock and Roll music? I would have to say Buddy Holly, Chuck Berry, Elvis, The Everly Brothers, Little Richard, Jerry Lee Lewis, Chubby Checker, and Bill Haley and His Comets. I wasn't around at that time. I'm born in 1960. I remember the Beatles quite distinctly, from "I Want To Hold Your Hand' and 'She Loves You' onward, but as a child.

The Beatles were highly influenced by Buddy Holly. In fact the name 'Beatles' is a homage to Buddy Holly. Holly's group was called, "The Crickets" presumably because they chirped. John Lennon changed the name of his group from The Quarrymen to "The Silver Beatles", a similar reference to insects as the Crickets, but with the cute pun 'beat' in the name, instead of spelling 'beetles' properly. 'Silver' was later dropped.

The term 'Rock and Roll' is actually a nautical phrase referring to the movement of a ship. The ship rocks to and fro, and rolls from side to side. So rock and roll music could just as easily have been termed, 'Rumble and sway', or 'olive dip and sesame paste' for that matter. It's all totally arbitrary.

The term "Rock and Roll" for the new musical style was coined in 1951 and invented by Cleveland radio host Alan Freed ('Moondog') who also played the new music constantly against all opposition, and even organized the first Rock Concert, The Moondog Coronation Ball on March 21st in the old Cleveland Arena. The authorities (Fire Department, Police, and other squares) shut it down even though over ten thousand people arrived for the sold-out show. Moondog tried again in Brooklyn New York, with, "Alan Freed's First Anniversary Rock and Roll Show". The term 'Rock and Roll' stuck. Before then it was called 'the big beat'.

Rock music evolved out of jazz, blues, country, gospel, and African music. When large numbers of African Americans left the rural areas and moved to urban centers the clash of cultures produced a fertile ground for musical overlap. There was an exchange of ideas and tastes. The middle-class kids of the cities took the fringe music of the streets and put it on the dinner table. It was still fringe until Bill Haley and His Comets' song, 'Rock Around the Clock' (1954) was used in the movie, "Blackboard Jungle" (1955). This started a craze and that song became the first mega-hit and brought rock and roll music to the world. Rock music was born. But Goree Carter had already recorded, 'Rock Awhile' with electric guitar (invented by Les Paul) in 1949, and 'Rock The Joint' by Jimmy Preston was also recorded in 1949. So Rock and Roll was not really invented, it developed. Little Richard says rock and roll is blues mixed with boogie.

Right at the point that the new fad, Rock and Roll Music, started to waver, and maybe would have indeed faded to oblivion, a new phenomena arrived just in time to save it. The British Invasion. A bunch of tough English Mods and Rockers on motorbikes (the Rockers had better motorbikes than the Mods but the Mods had better clothes) started making music of their own. So to the shores of the colonies arrived The Beatles, The Kinks, The Rolling Stones, The Who, The Animals, The Moody Blues, The Zombies, The Dave Clark 5, Herman's Hermits, The Yardbirds, and others to save the day.

The Brits had aquired the new music a bit later than the kids who were inventing it. It took time to assimilate it. Then to create music of their own that was inspired by it. So by the time the Beatles had the Mersey Beat ready to take overseas, the fad had lost some of its momentum. The British Invasion arrived just in time.

Then in the late 60s when that wave lost its momentum, the Hippies in California (Jefferson Airplane, Grateful Dead, in San Francisco and The Doors in Los Angeles and others) came to revive it.

Then in the early 70s when that wave lost its momentum, Hard Rock (Led Zeppelin, Deep Purple and others), Southern Rock (Allman Brothers, Marshall Tucker Band, and others), and Progressive Rock (Yes, Renaissance, and others) came to revive it.

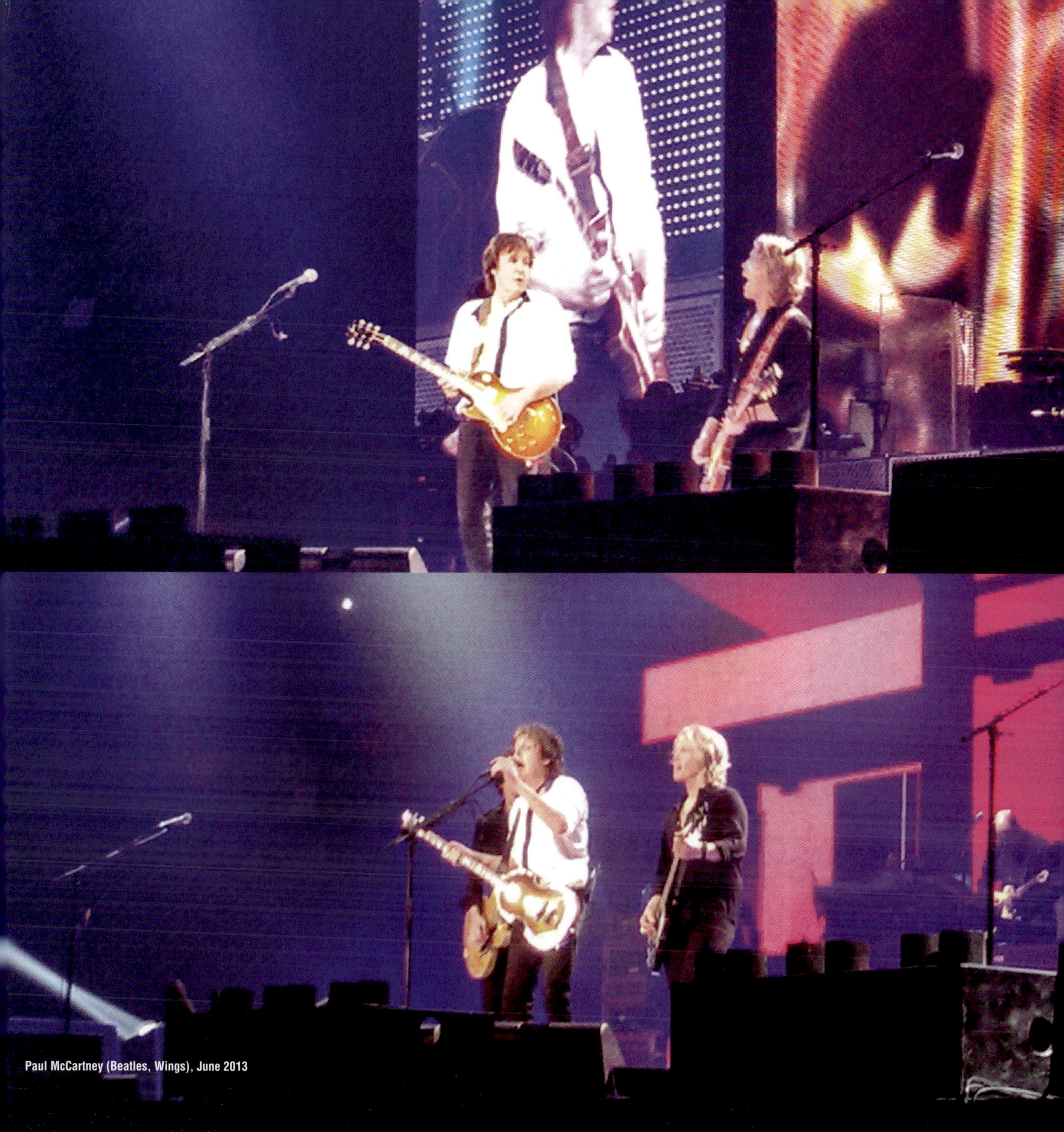

Paul McCartney (Beatles, Wings), June 2013

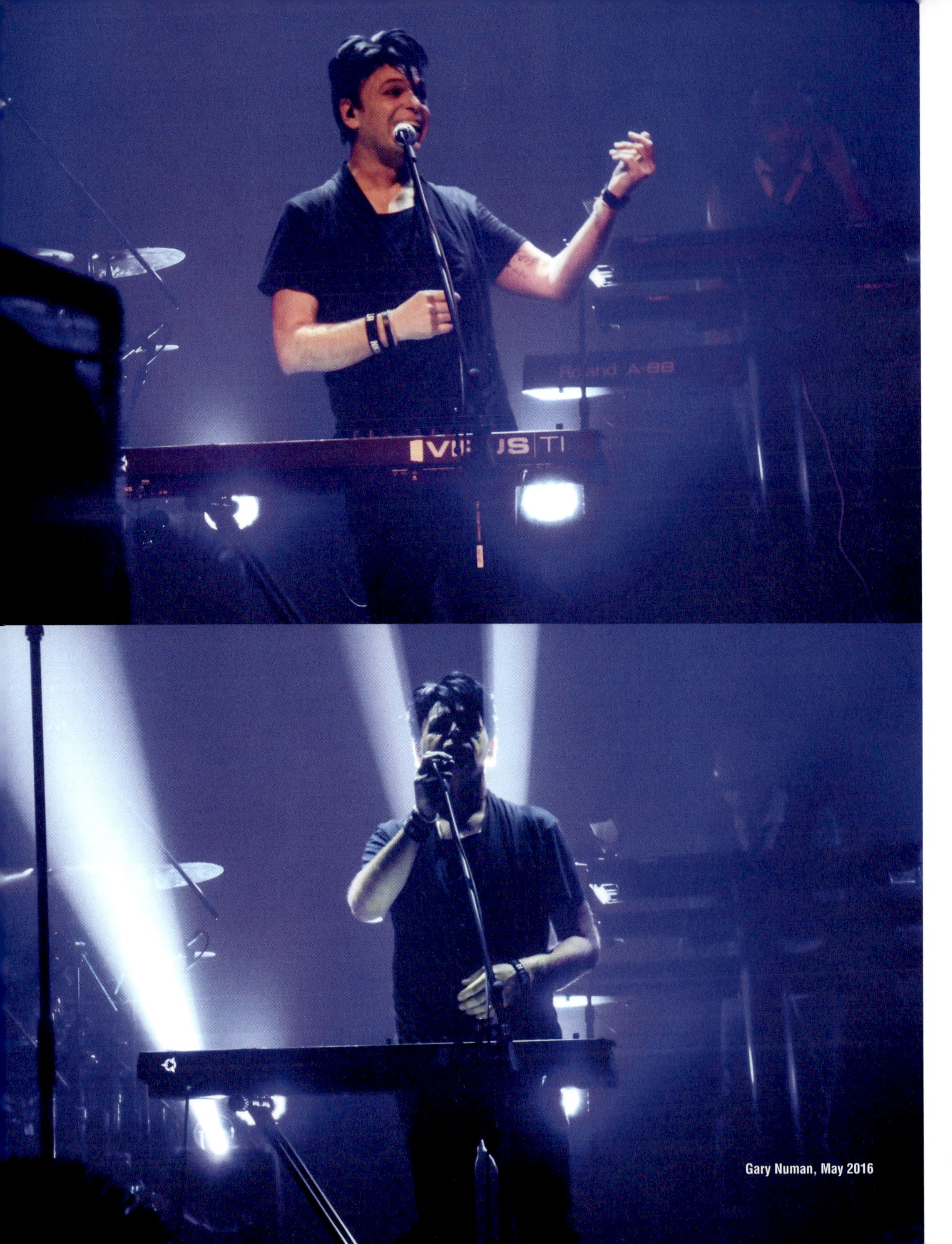

Gary Numan, May 2016

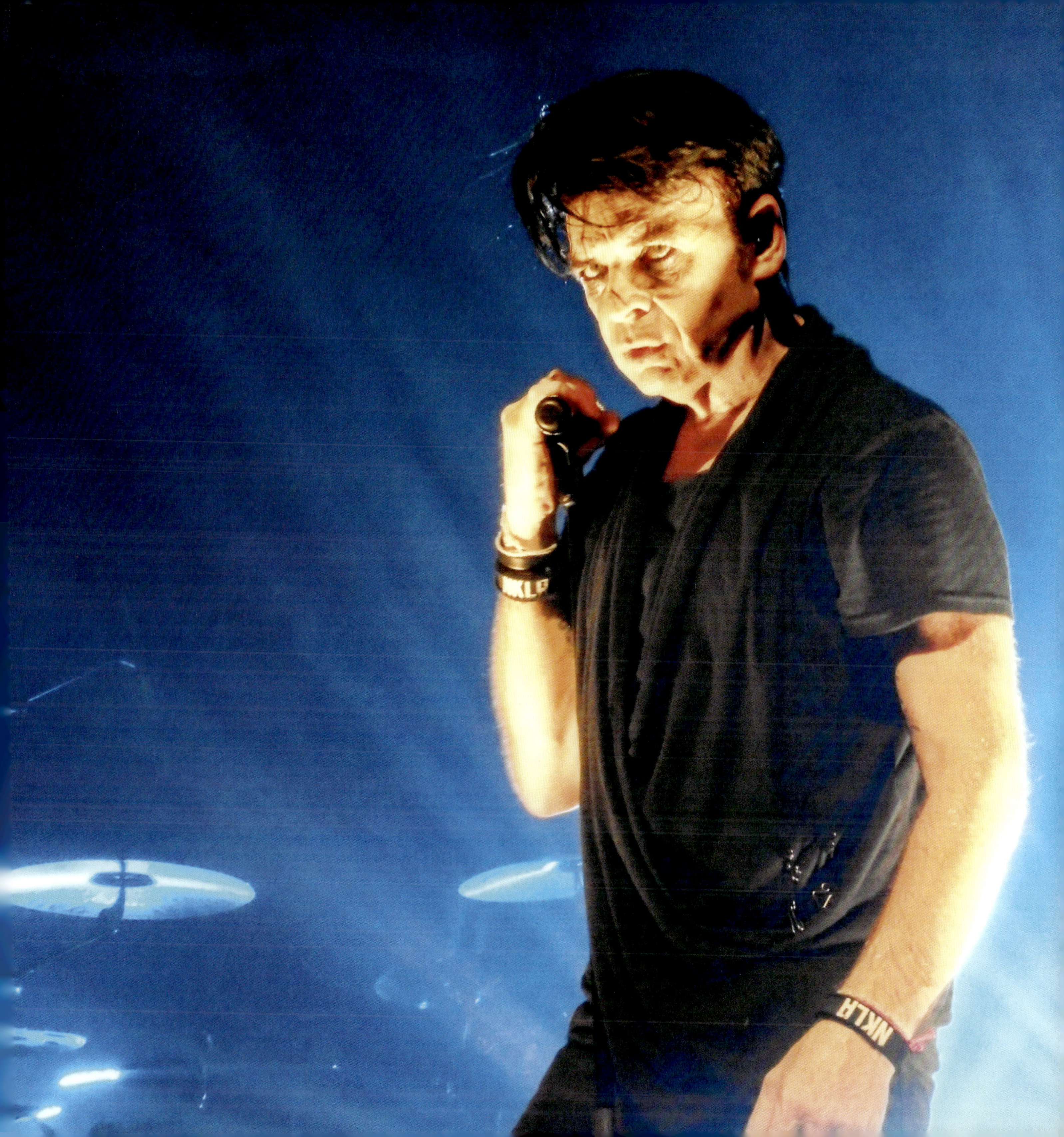

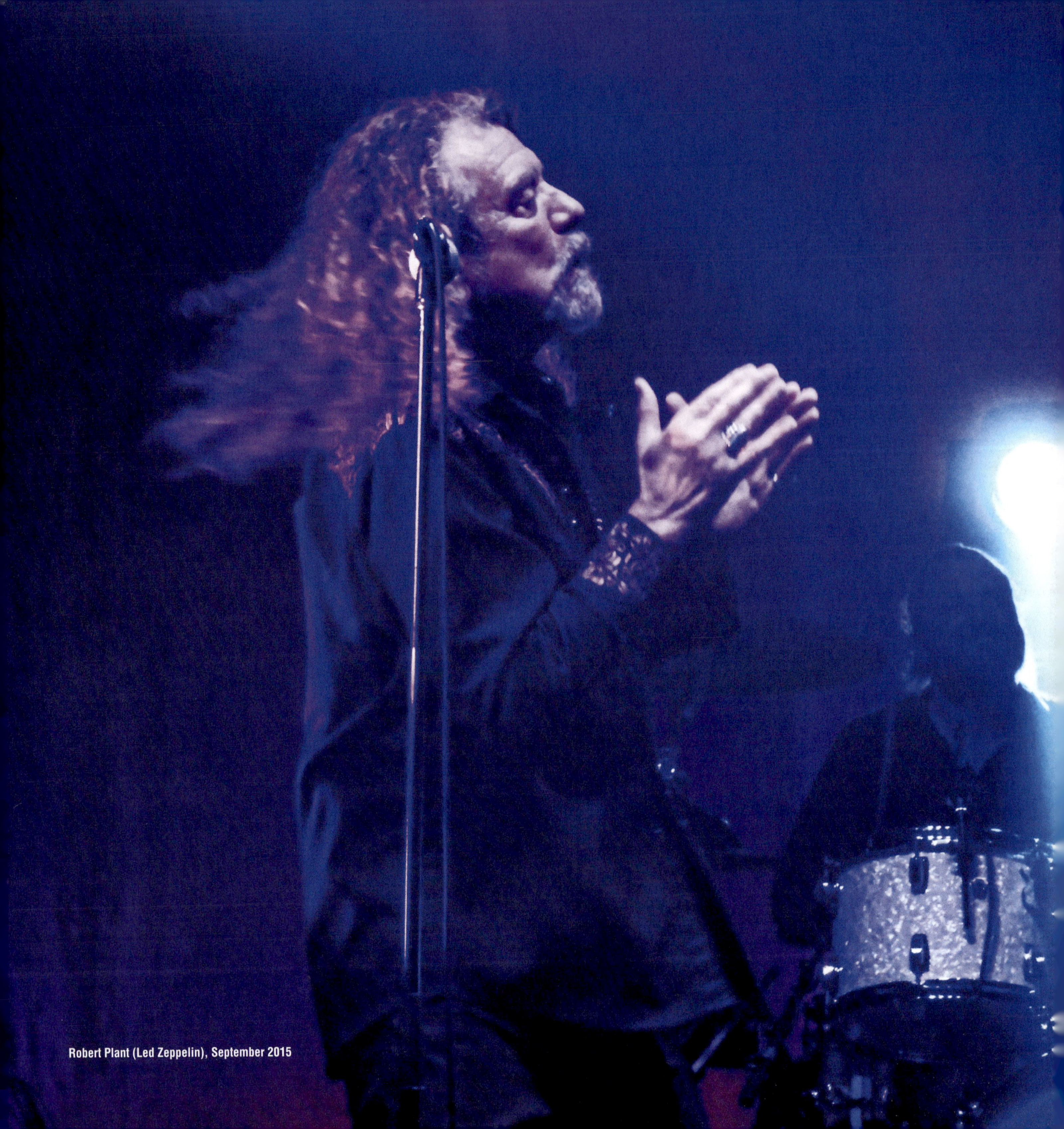

Robert Plant (Led Zeppelin), September 2015

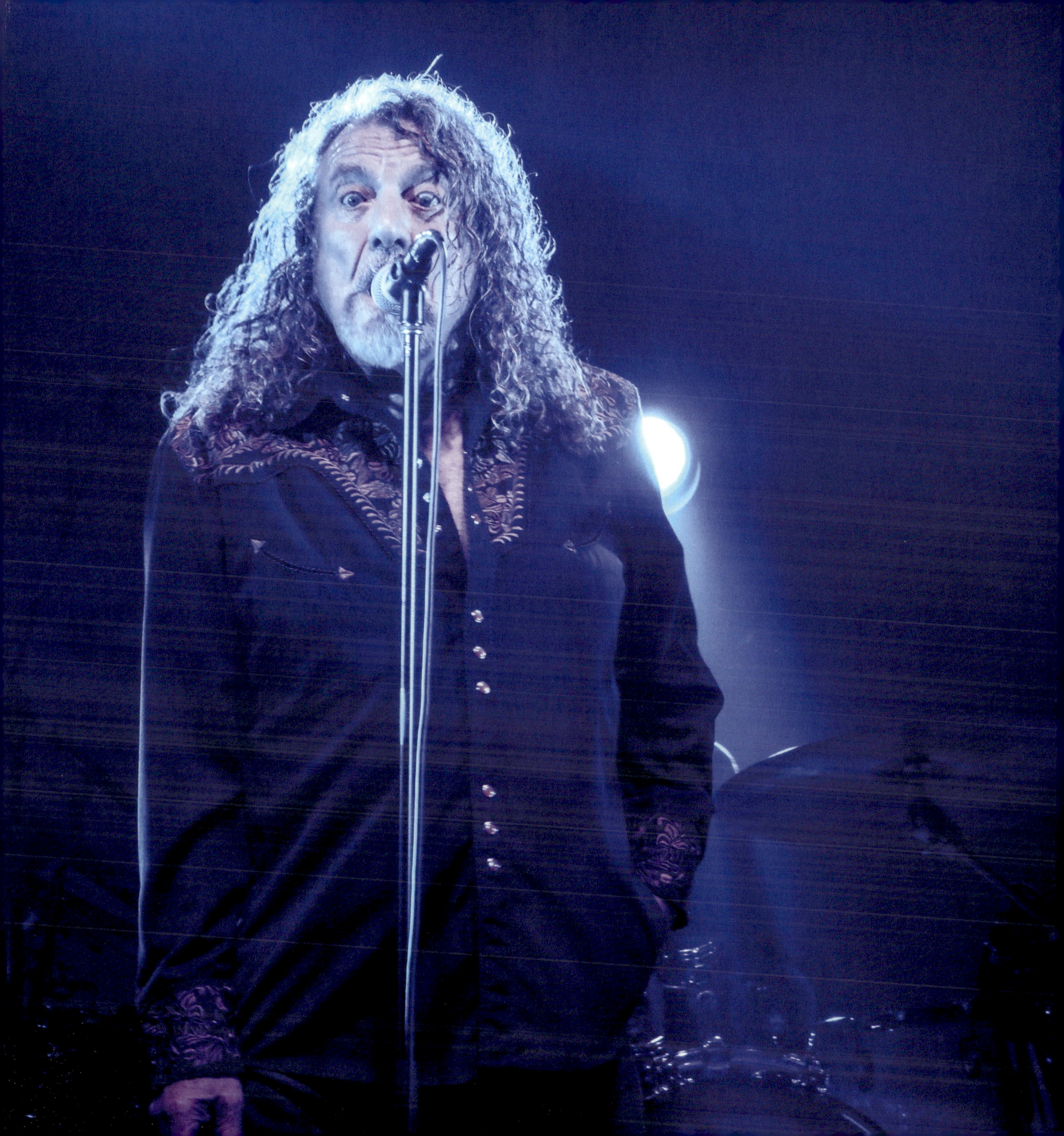

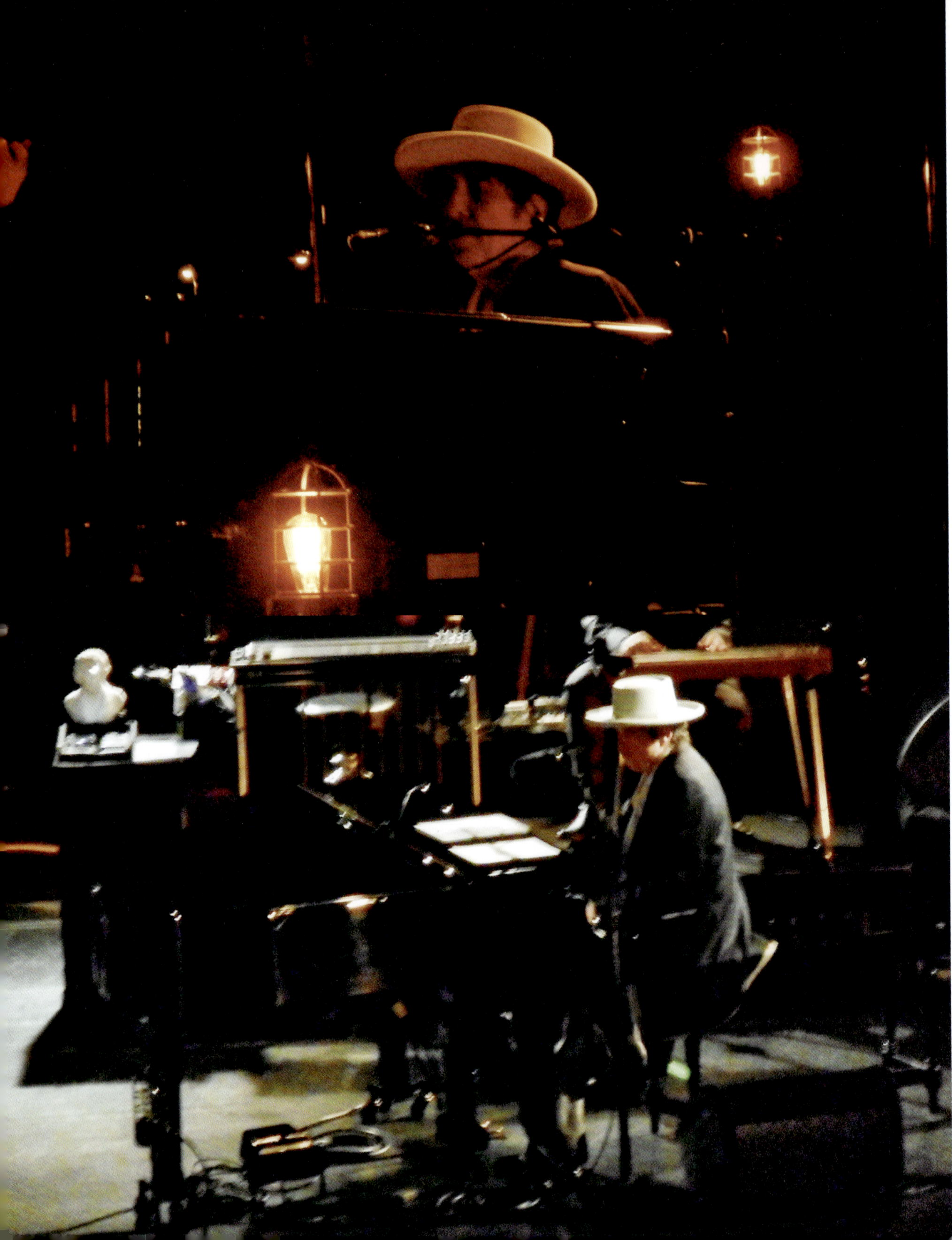

Bob Dylan, November 2014

Then in the mid 70s when that wave hadn't even lost its momentum yet, Glam Rock (David Bowie, T-rex) and Punk (Sex Pistols and others from England), and New Wave (straight out of New York- the Ramones, Patti Smith, Blondie, The Talking Heads, and others).

By now rock music was too well established to be thought of as a fad. We did it. We created a new art form. Theater has been around for thousands of years, and opera for hundreds of years. Rock and Roll is still new, but it's here to stay. So did Rock music start as a fad? The answer is it slowly developed from the late 1940s to the early 1950s, then became a big fad, but then continued to develop, and is developing still.

And that's why this is an historic moment in history, because many of the inventors and originators of rock music are still alive and well and on stage, even in their 60s, 70s, and even 80s. Full of energy and talent and whipping the crowd into a frenzy. Only the crowd is a bunch of old geezers like me and not 17-year-old kids. They can't go on like this much longer.

I saw BB King and Jerry Lee Lewis (separately) perform on stage when they were in their 80s. They were great but they had noticeably slowed down. Pete Seegar (RIP) was in his 90s the last time I saw him perform. A few songs and go home. Pete and BB are no longer with us. But the Who, and Patti Smith are still playing two hour shows and exploding with energy. This is it.

If you go to a concert of a group that started in the 50s, like The Platters or The Drifters, you will today see not one of the original members. They have been replaced one by one. You will see members who were in the band at the same time as original members, but no original members left. But if you go see a group of the 60s and 70s, you will see original members. They have not been all replaced. Yet. So the question is... How much longer?

In 1965 Mick Jagger was interviewed on British television.

Interviewer: "You've been doing this for how long?"

Mick: "Two years."

"How much longer do you give yourself doing this thing, being a sort of, of..."

"I don't know, I never thought I'd be doing it for two years even. When we started off I never thought we'd make it very big anyway. I don't know, I think we're pretty well set up for at least another year."

Another year? The interviewer was really asking, "How much longer are you going to waste your time goofing off with this nonsense and go get a real job? Ok, it's good for a lark. There's obviously no future in it."

And Mick answers, "at least another year", meaning, "hey, I'm enjoying the now, not worried about the future. We're artists. We don't worry about tomorrow."

When I became a long-haired teenager and started going to concerts, the 70s were in full swing. I didn't really see the birth of Rock and Roll but I did witness the birth of "New Wave" which came on the heels of punk rock. I saw the rise of Blondie, Talking Heads, Patti Smith, and The Ramones, and the purity and joy that they brought along.

I saw the Talking Heads in 1977 just before their first album came out. They played all the songs from that album and it was amazing. I joined the Talking Heads fan club. When the album finally came out shortly afterwards, it was totally innovative and remains one of my favorite albums to this day (Talking Heads '77). I recently saw David Byrne in concert and he was great but only performed one Talking Heads song, "Road to Nowhere", as an encore. He's still great and making excellent music, but he's just not doing that anymore. All great artists are constantly evolving and creating. And you never know what your next great hit will be. Audiences are fickle. In show business you have to keep reinventing yourself.

Santana had two number one hits from their 1999 album, Supernatural. 'Smooth' and 'Maria Maria' both topped the charts. Their last number one hit had been in 1971. Twenty-eight years between number one hits, a Guinness World Record. The Grateful Dead didn't have a top forty hit until 1987, when 'Touch of Grey' hit number 9. So next time you go to a concert and only want to hear 'their old stuff', remember, the old stuff was new once too. Still, a group should also play some of their old stuff; that's what you came to hear.

When I saw the Talking Heads, this was something new. Up until then I had seen the following concerts in order, Jefferson Starship (free in Central Park 1976), The Allman Brothers (Nassau Colliseum1977), The Who (with Keith Moon, Madison Square Garden 1977), the Grateful Dead (Englishtown NJ 1977).

So at age 17 to see the Talking Heads after all that was a revelation. I mean they were YOUNG. All the other groups were guys in their 30s. Old guys. The Heads were more or less my generation. What a bunch of crazies with David Byrne at the helm. I went over to them at the end of the show (in the auditorium at New York University in Greenwich Village) and spoke to them for a while. I told David, "I've seen some great groups. You guys are going to be big."

But there were many great groups that didn't become big. Like Susan Springfield and the Erasers. But the Talking Heads had something the Erasers didn't have. A lucky break. The Heads got to do two songs from their second album on Saturday Night Live. After that their career took off. I witnessed this with my own eyes.

So is it luck or talent? Well, fortune favors the bold. If you've really got talent and you can stick with it and push and work, the luck will eventually come. So it's not luck at all.

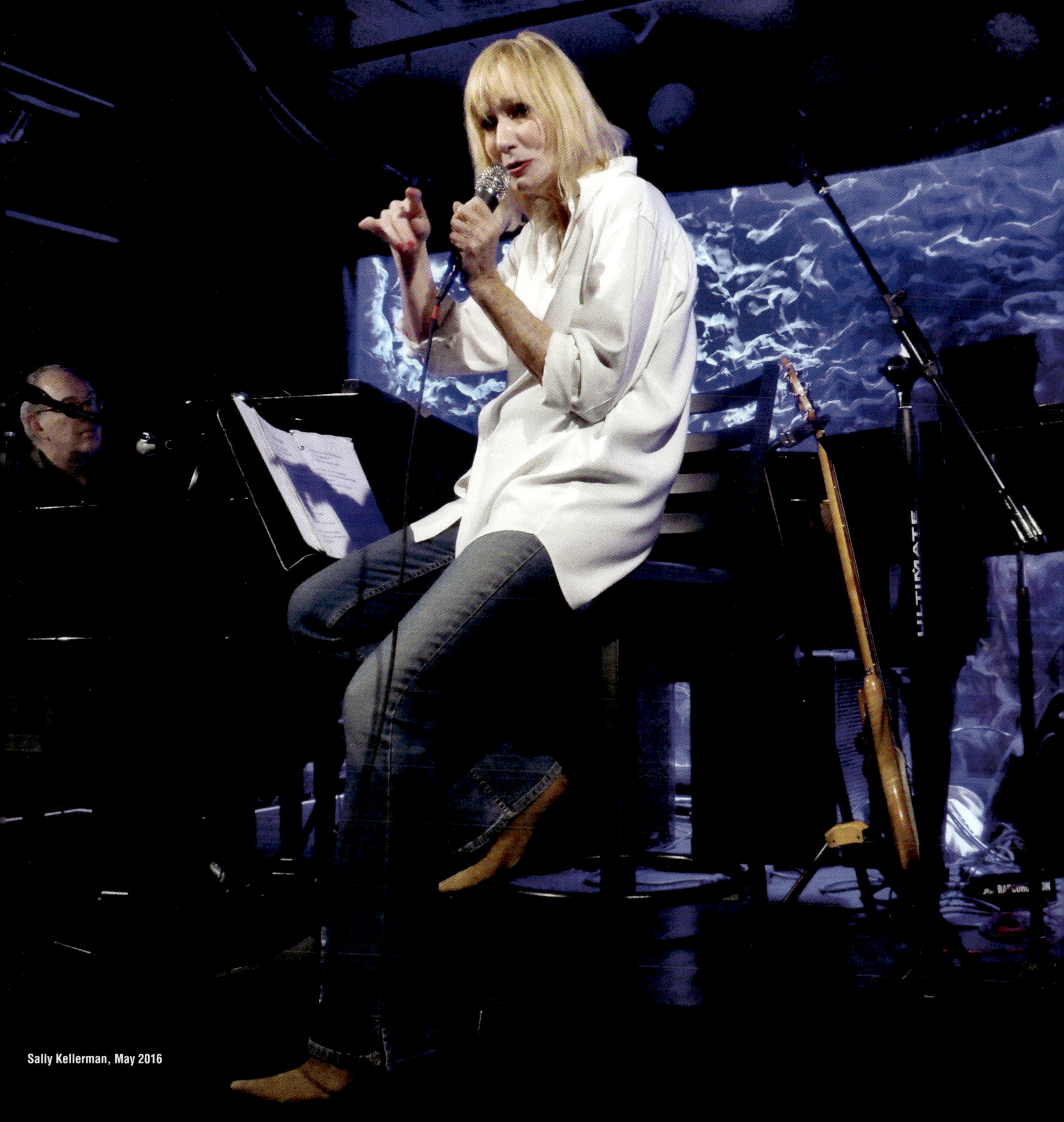

Sally Kellerman, May 2016

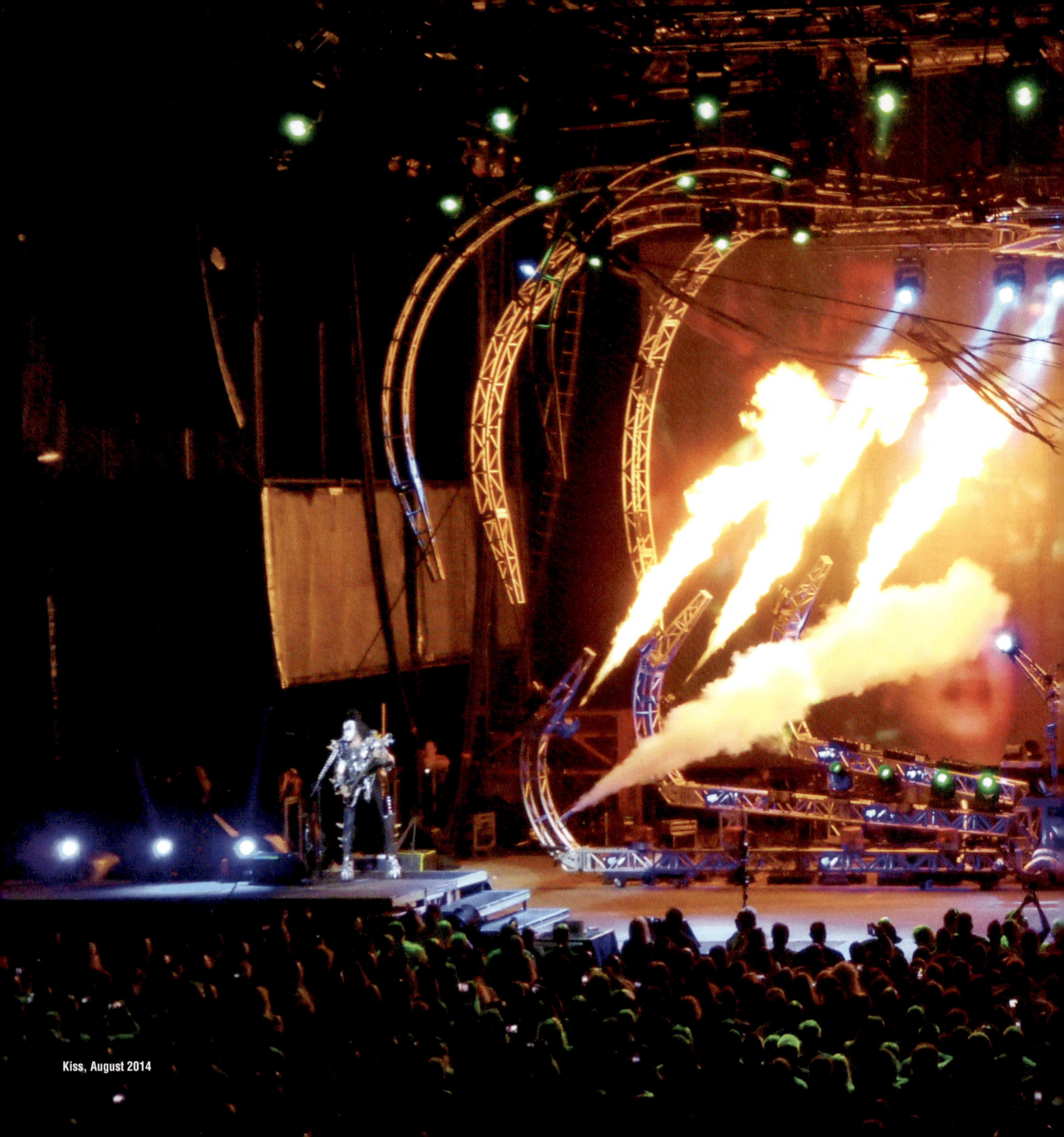

Kiss, August 2014

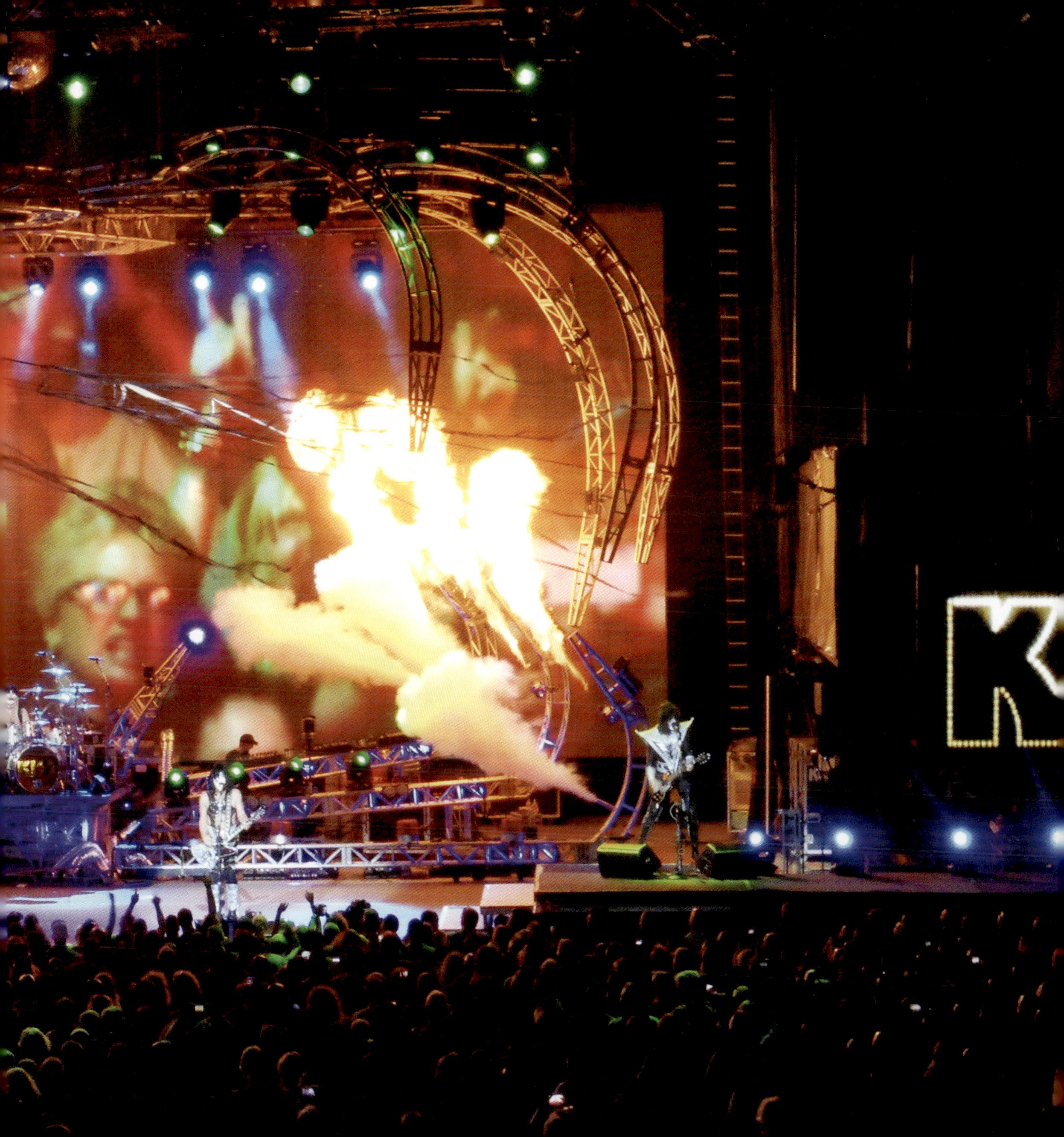

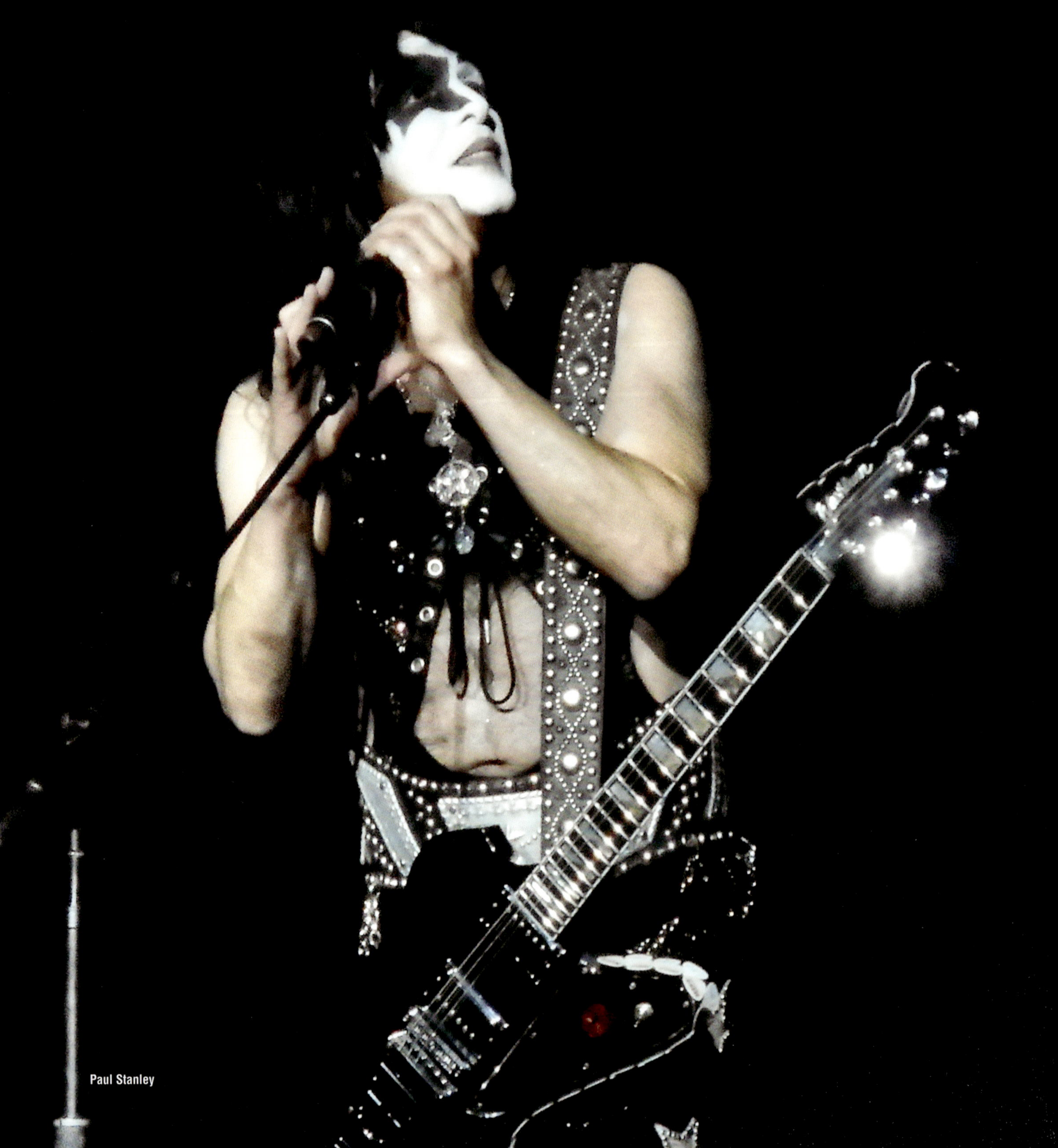

Paul Stanley

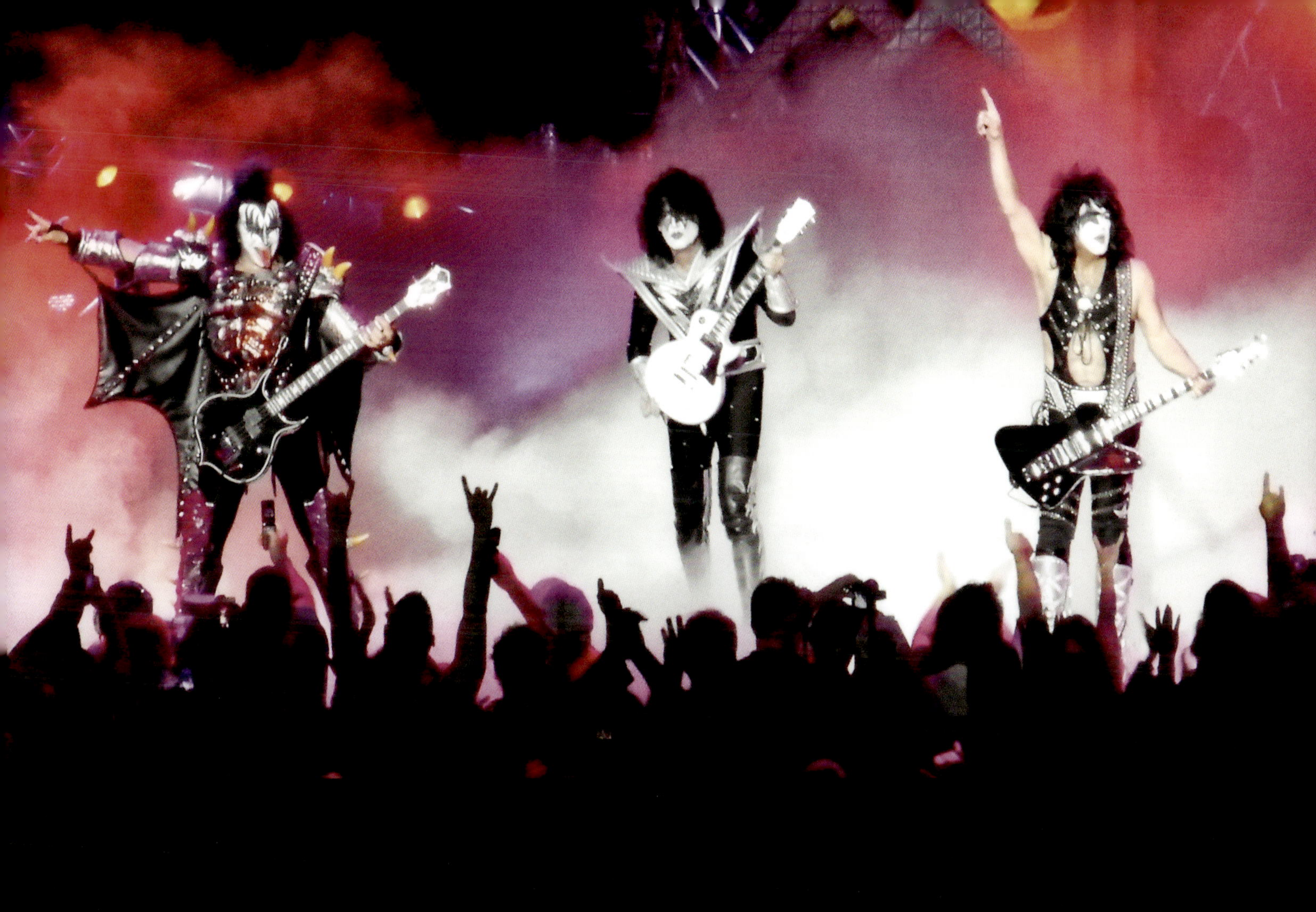

Kiss members, Gene Simmons, Tommy Thayer, Paul Stanley

Rock music is constantly changing. It is a living organism. And everyone thinks that the music of their generation (their teenage years, the power years), are the best. Our parents couldn't stand the Beatles (for the most part). Is anyone truly open-minded? Even James Bond said (in Goldfinger), 'oh you can't serve the wine like that, that would be almost as bad as listening to the Beatles without earmuffs.'

Seeing the Talking Heads at this time, the B52s, Patti Smith, the Shirts, it was all so new and happening. But when there wasn't anything else to do and we wanted to go do something, we went to see our default band. The Ramones. Who knew they would become legendary? And influential. How influential? They were the Picasso of Rock bands. They did it new, and great, and there were many that followed and imitated, but didn't do it nearly as well. So the others were not only an imitation, but a poor one at that. A million Ramones imitators that stunk. Stank. Stanka. What a mess. Picasso could get away with drawing abstract painting because he invented it and knew what he was doing. But walk into most art galleries and museums today? Mostly junk.

Trying to be like Picasso and failing miserably. Then, every once in a while someone comes along and isn't trying to be like someone else, rather is just expressing himself or herself artistically and it's sublime.

If the Ramones were the Picasso of our generation, then Pete Townsend is the Mozart (1756-1791). Or the Beethoven (1770-1827). Notice the overlap? Pete has the creative energy of the classical music heroes, but just as Pete said, "Hope I die before I get old", Mozart actually did it. But fortunately Pete is still going strong, full of energy, happily tearing up the guitar with his front-man Roger. Fifty years after singing, "This is my generation", they are still singing it, full of energy and filling the stadiums. Our rock legends, the creators of rock music, are still with us. Don't miss an opportunity to go see them. And take pictures.

If Pete is the Mozart, what are The Beatles? The Beatles are Franz Liszt (1811-1886). Why? When the Beatles started out there were millions of screaming girls watching them and following them around and fainting and weeping. This was similar to how the fans used to react to seeing Franz Liszt on stage playing piano. Doctors were making house calls to an entire generation of hysterical girls who had glimpsed Franz and could no longer function. They were swooning in bed for months. The new ailment was termed, "Lisztomania".

"I'm sorry to tell you this sir, but your daughter is suffering from Lisztomania".

"Oh dear".

"You must tell your wife the bad news".

"I can't, she's got it too."

When girls had similar symptoms in 1964, they called it "Beatlemania".

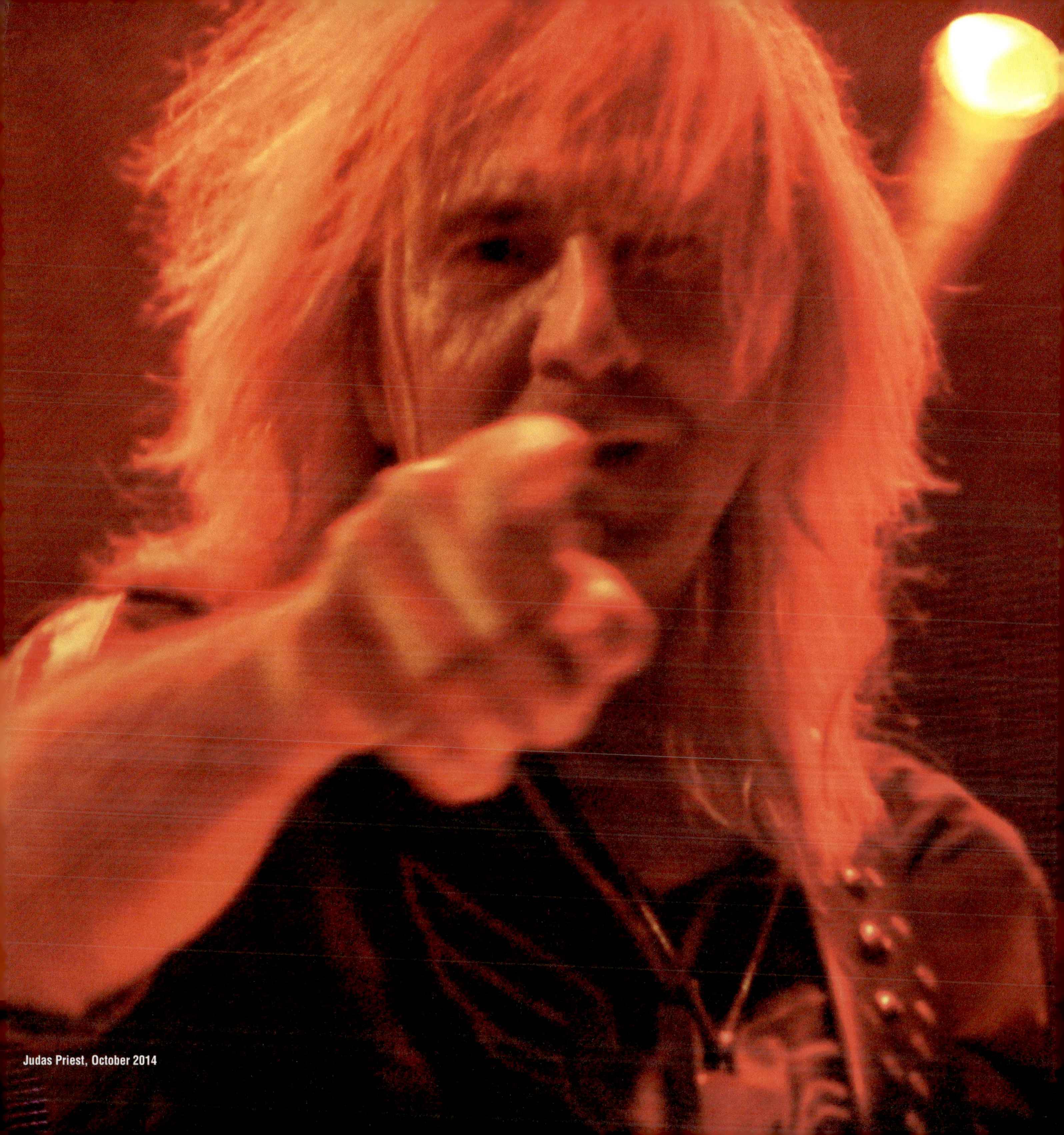
Judas Priest, October 2014

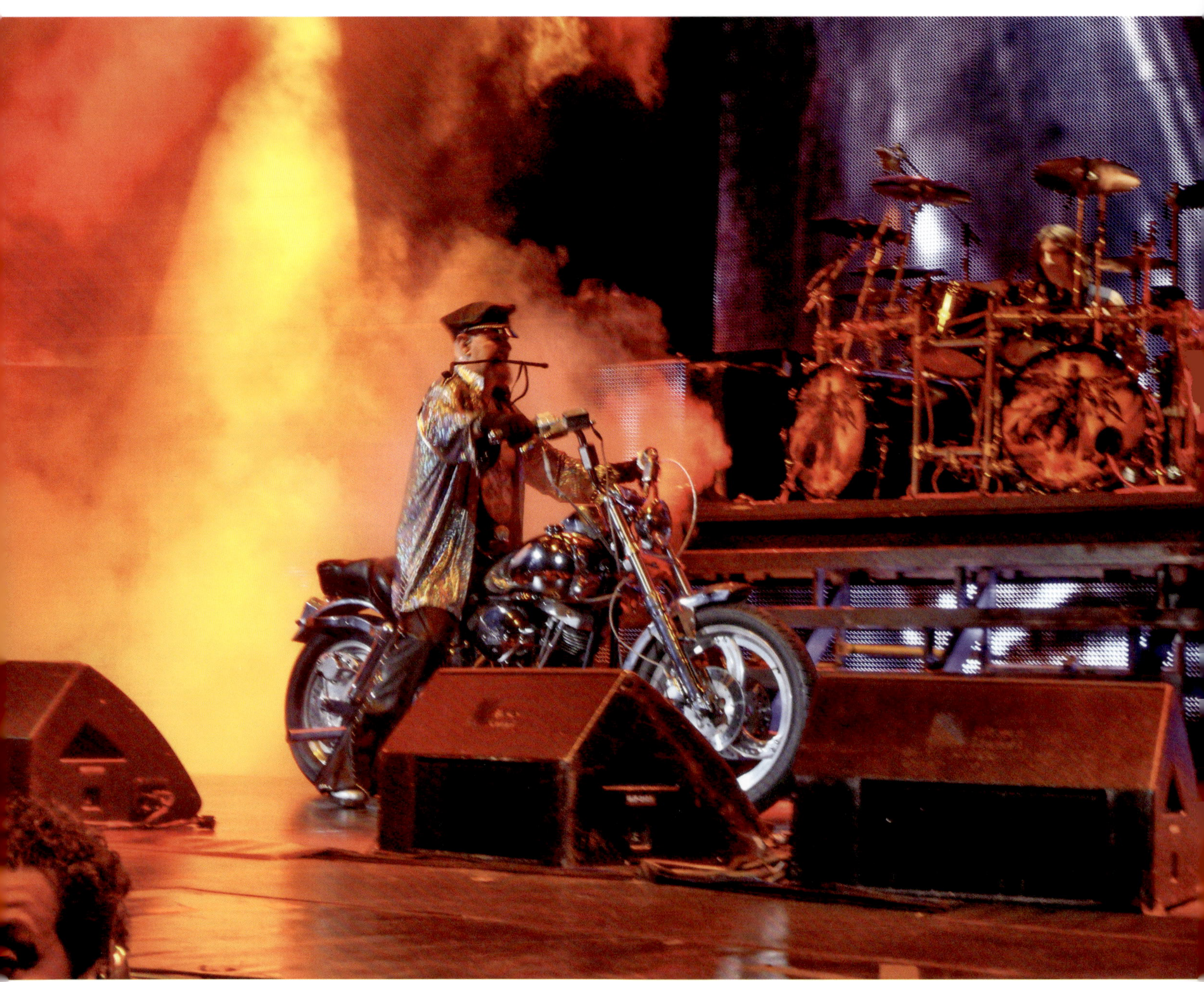

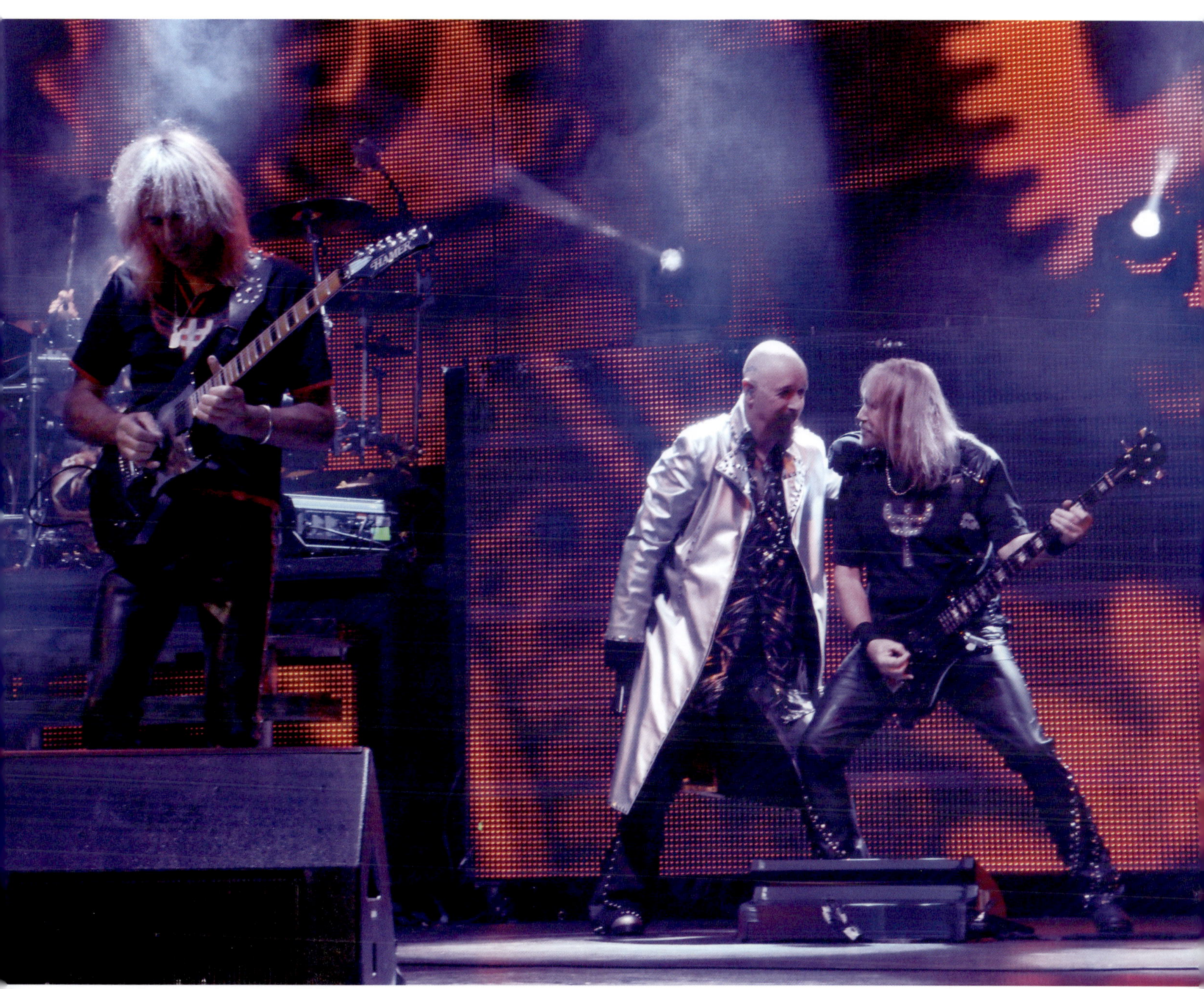

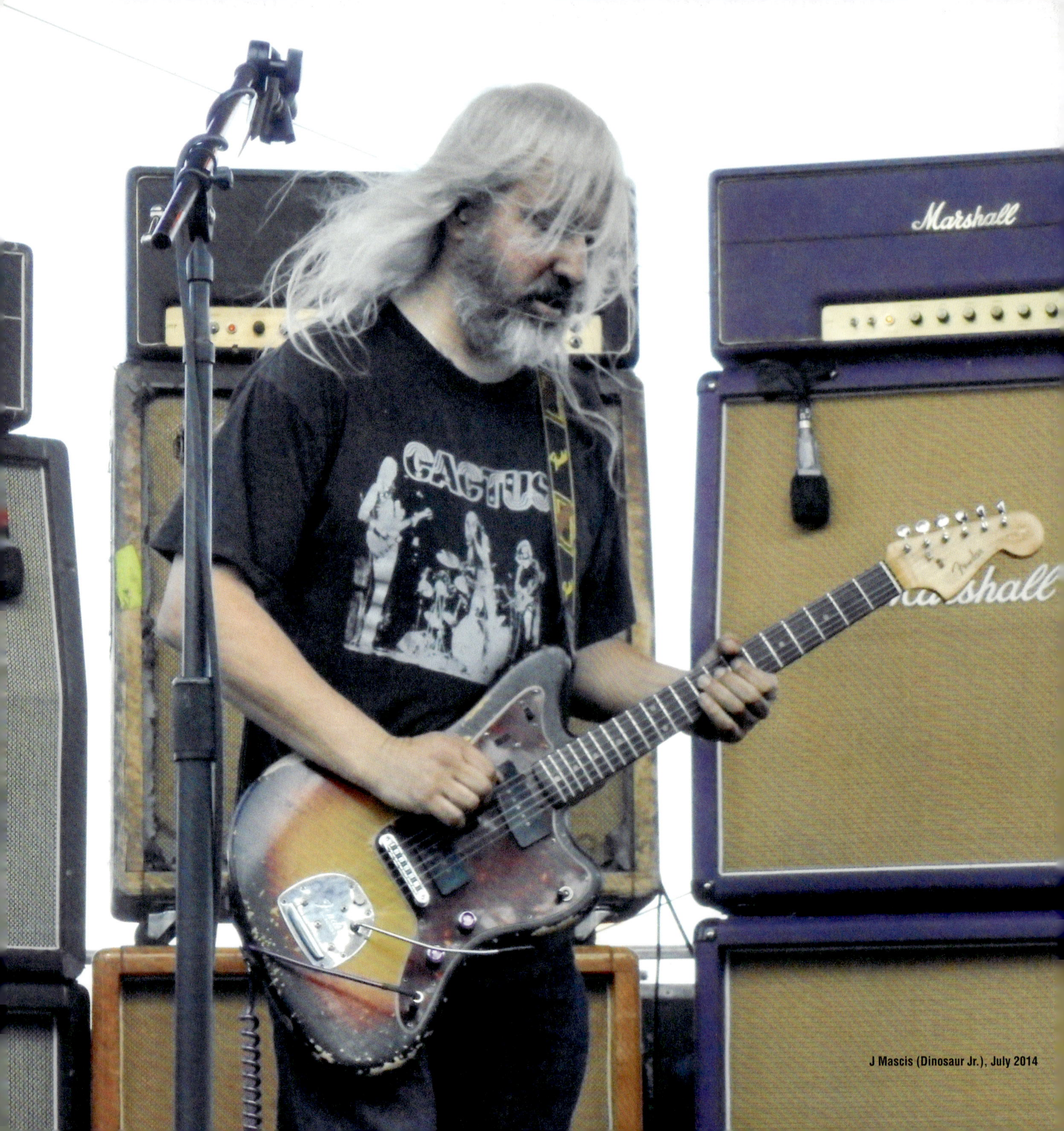

J Mascis (Dinosaur Jr.), July 2014

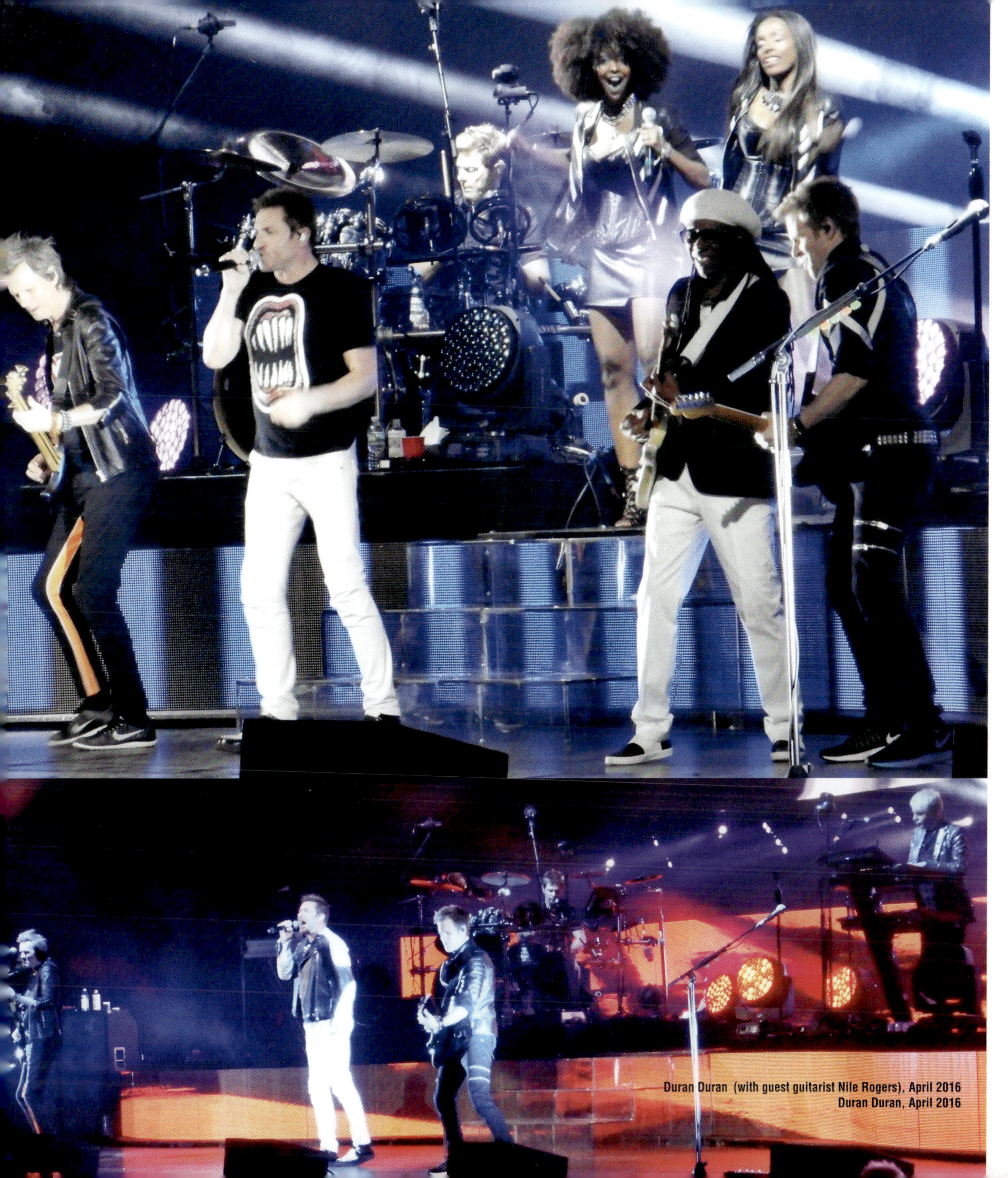

Duran Duran (with guest guitarist Nile Rogers), April 2016
Duran Duran, April 2016

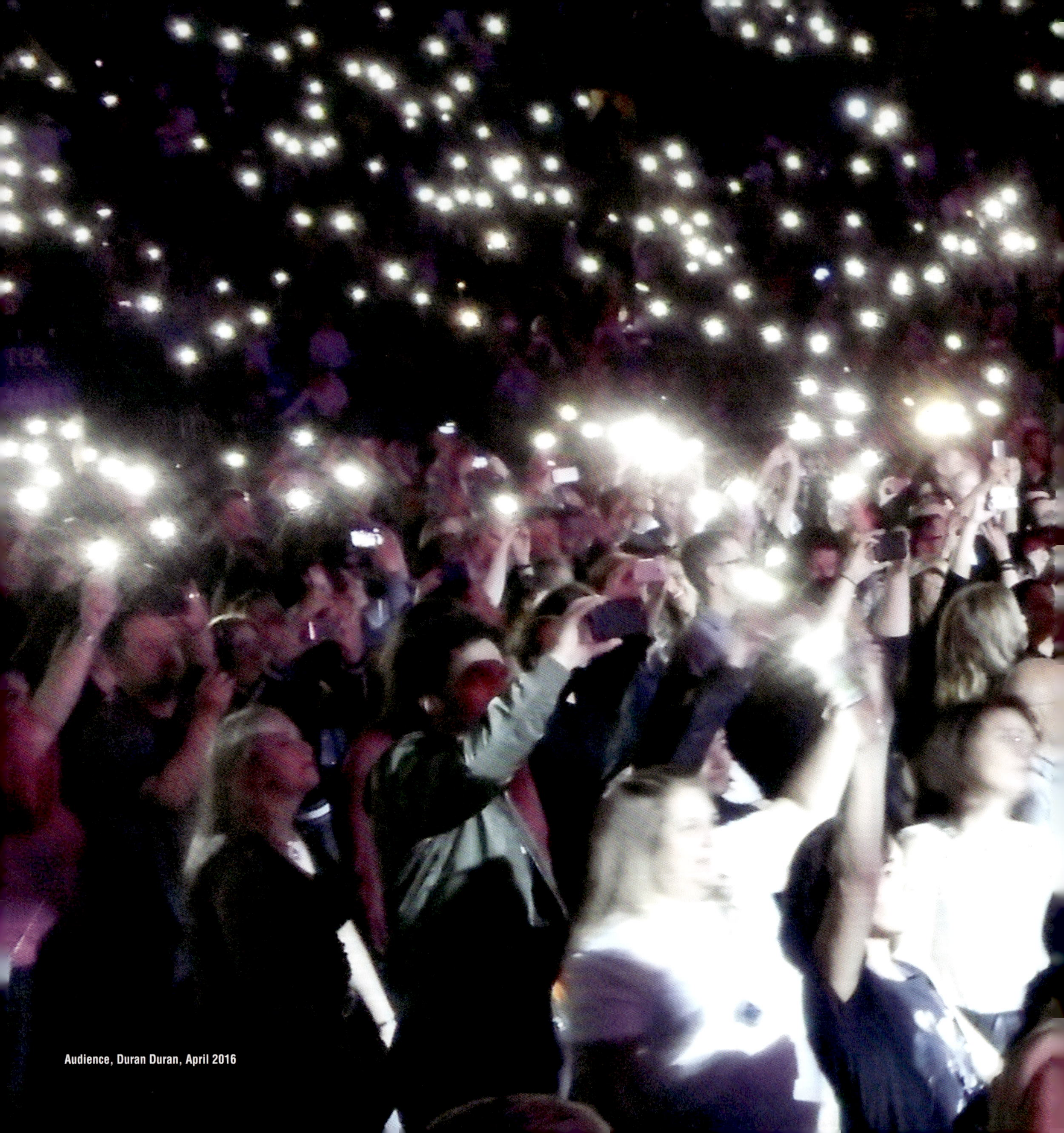

Audience, Duran Duran, April 2016

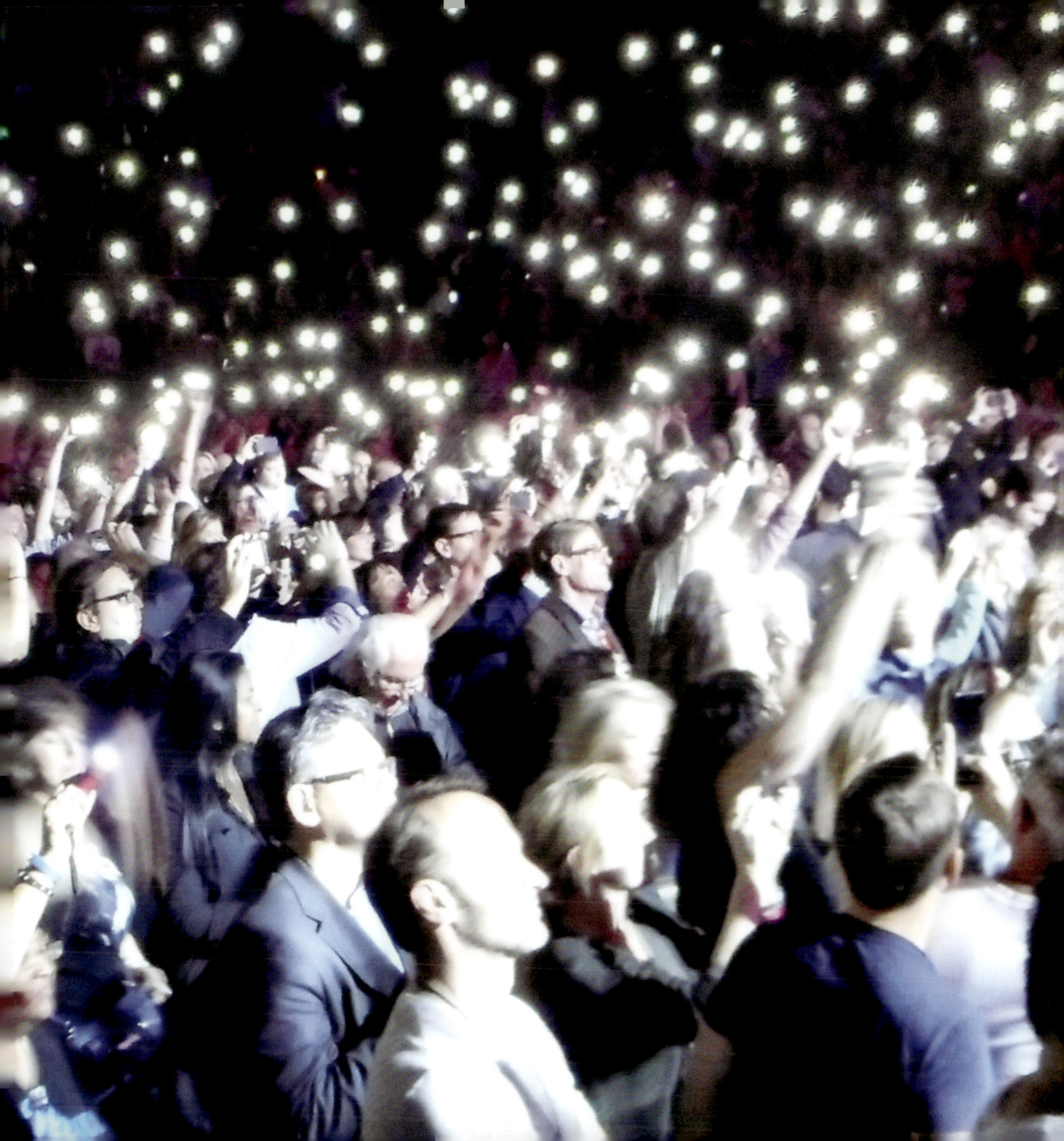

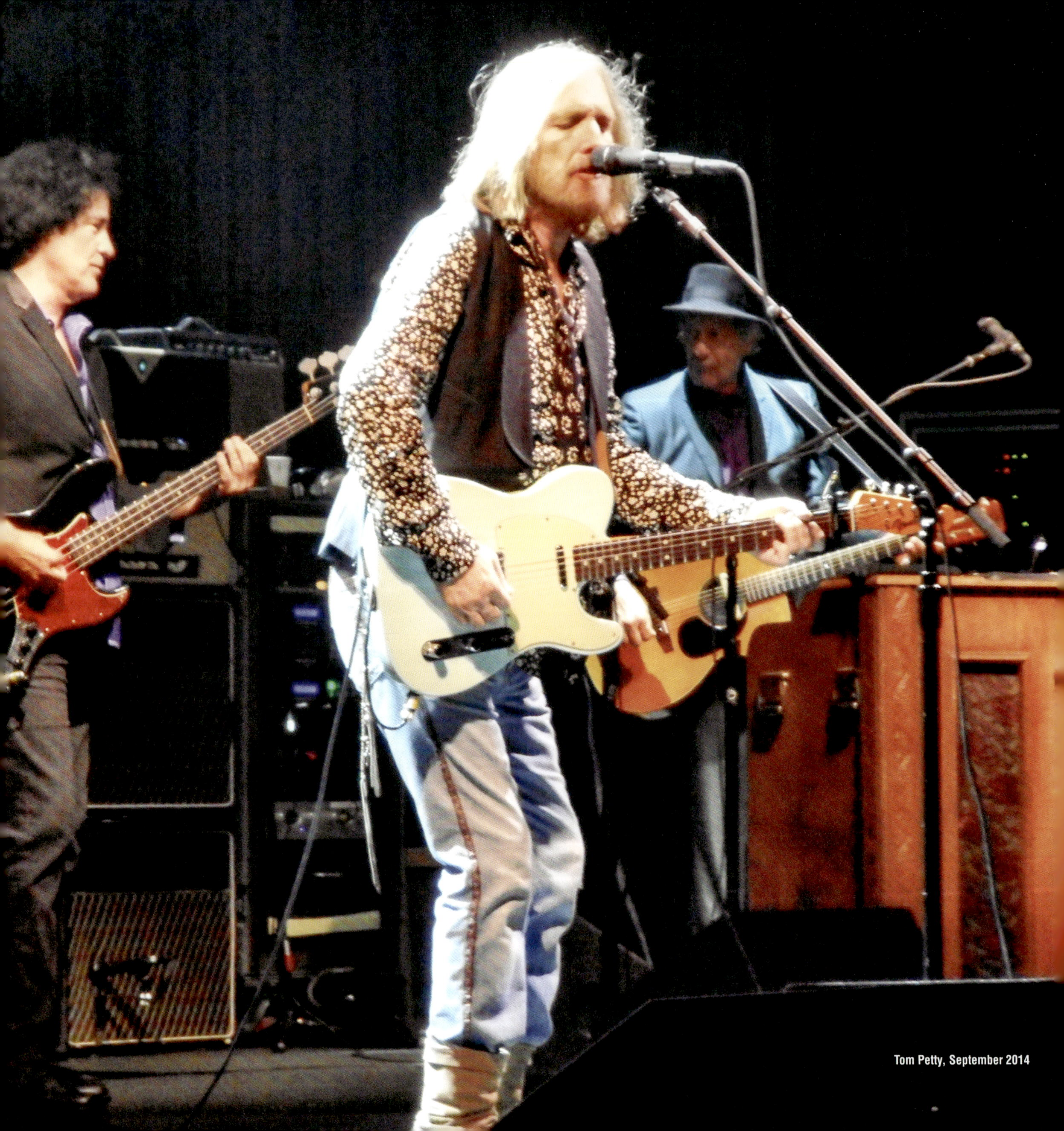
Tom Petty, September 2014

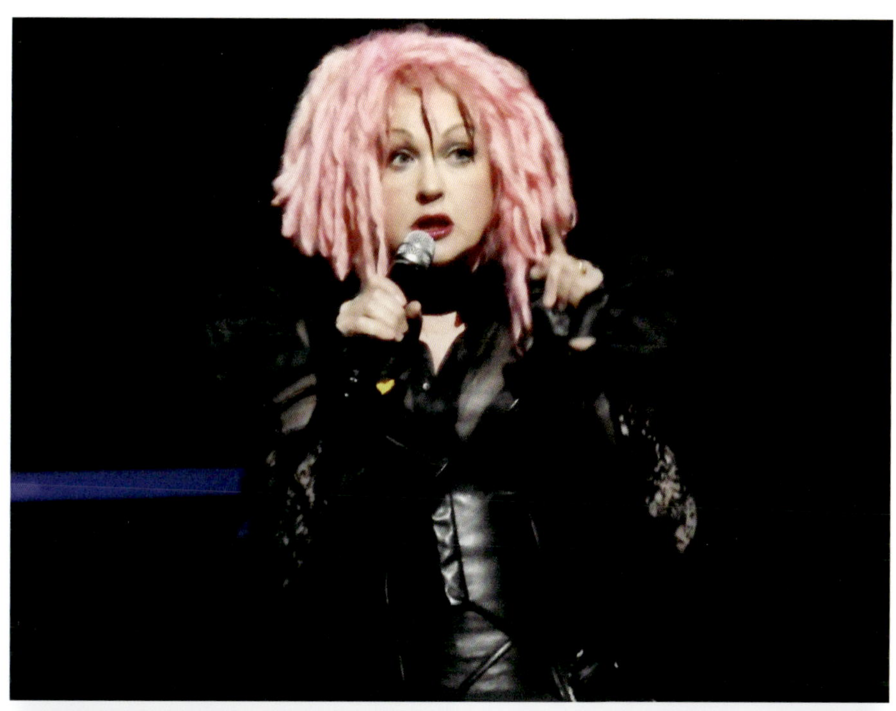

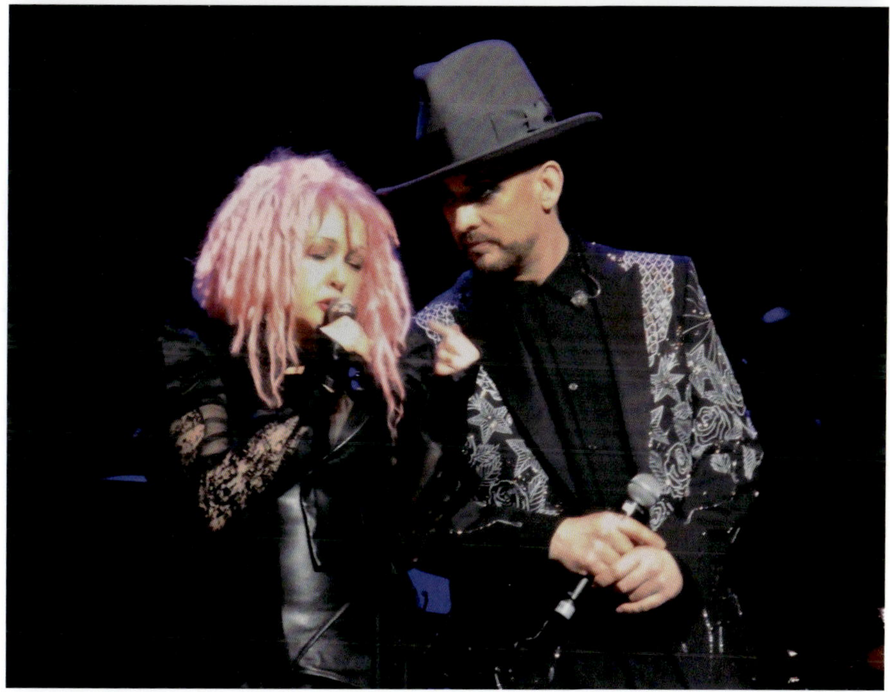

Cyndi Lauper, May 2016

Cyndi Lauper and Boy George, May 2016

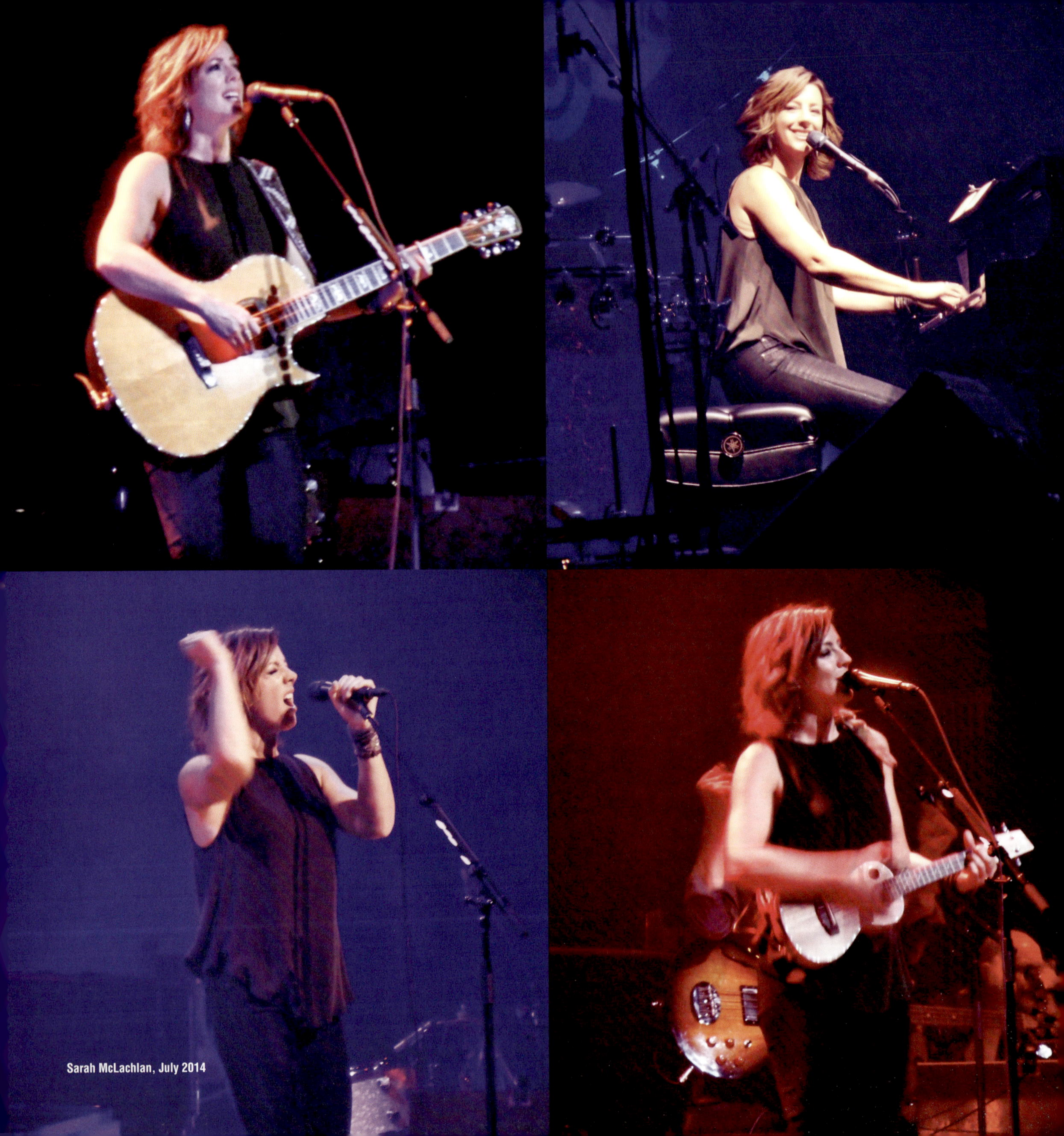

Sarah McLachlan, July 2014

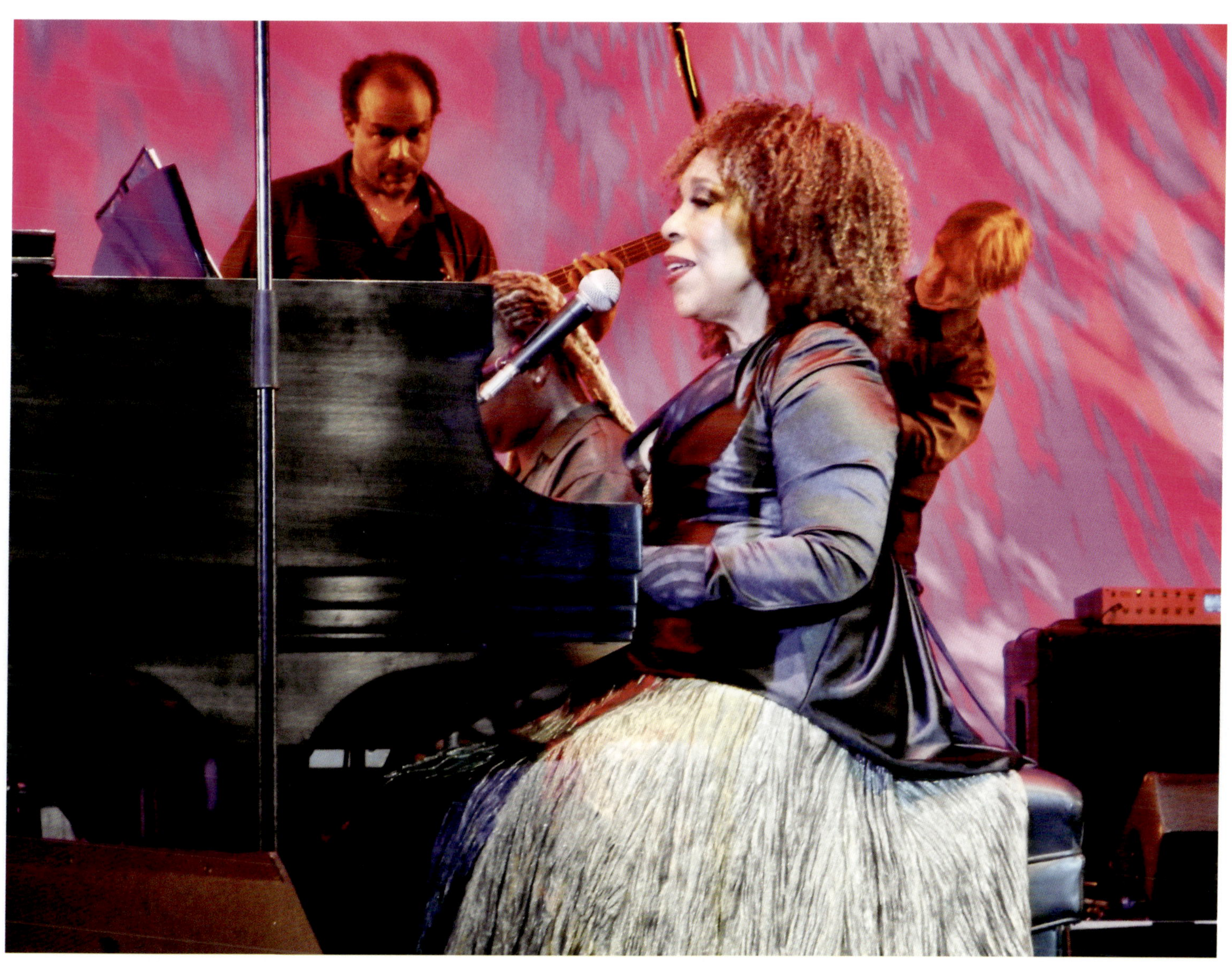

Roberta Flack, July 2014

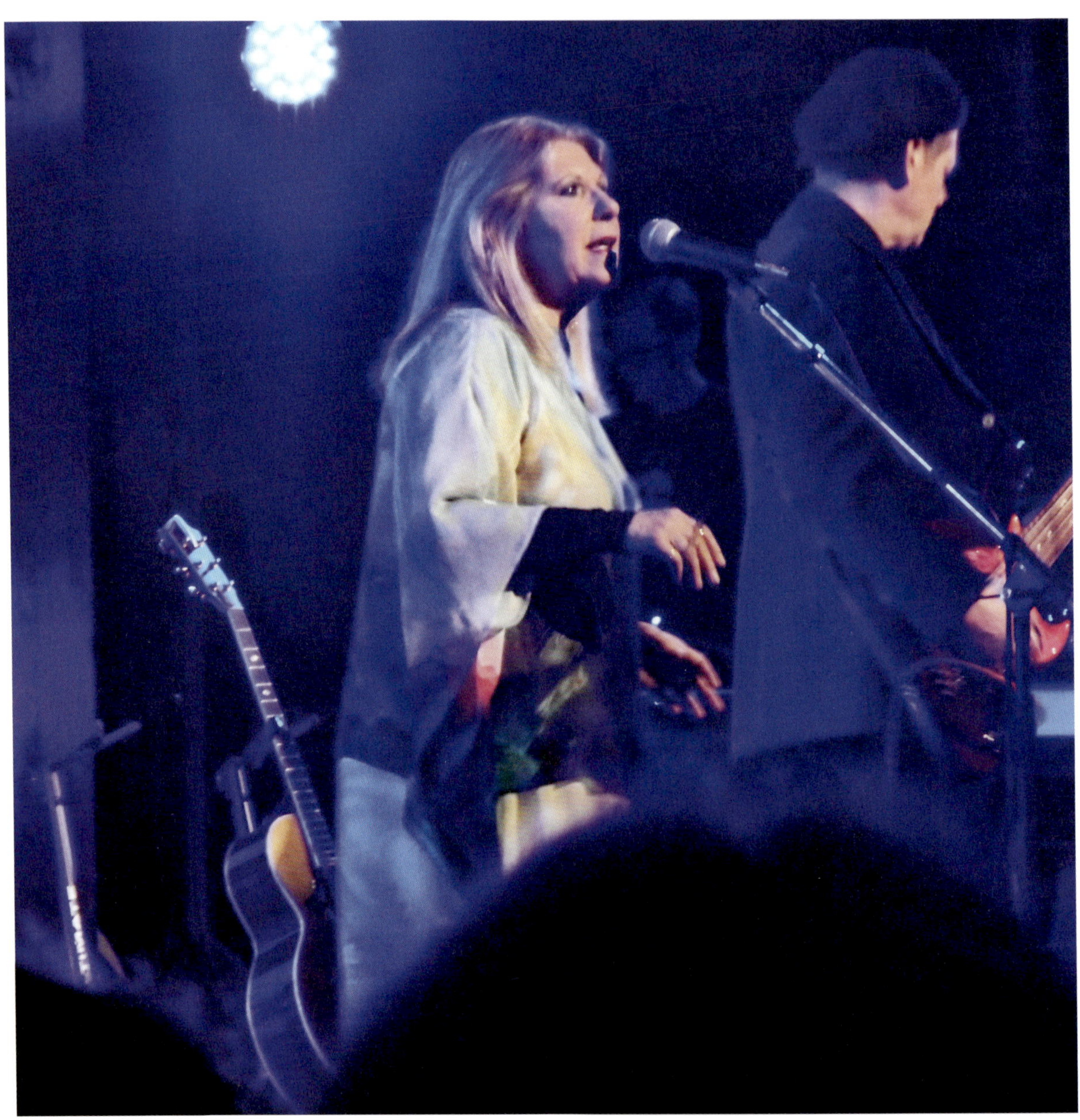

Annie Haslam (Renaissance), October 2014

The Talking Heads. They weren't 60s music. They were now. It was still the 60s up until then. The 60s didn't end on December 31st, 1969. It went on for a few years, politically and musically. In fact, why we arbitrarily call the 60s- ''the 60s'' is beyond me. Can't you come up with a better name? No one called The Renaissance- 'the 90s. If they had it would have ended on December 31st, 1499. And then no Raphael and Titian?

But still, for no particular reason it's natural to break down periods of time into groupings for the sake of organization, and groupings of ten are logical. And for a very good reason. Because we have ten fingers. That's why. So it has a reason, but it's still arbitrary.

I have some pictures of Blondie here and Debbie Harry looks and sounds great. The last time I saw Blondie was in 1979. Then 34 years later I go see her and she's still working the crowd up into a frenzy. They played The Highline Ballroom in Times Square which is a great venue for a rock concert. You can sit back and relax if you want, on chairs in the balcony, you can dance at the back of the floor, or if you have the energy and chutzpah you can inch your way to the front row and stand on the floor. I find it worthwhile to suffer through all the misery and push (politely) to the front. There are the crazies, there are the fanatics, and there are the hardcore fans. I did this once in 1978 at the Rolling Stones in Cleveland Ohio's sports stadium. 83 thousand people and I had to push (politely) to the front and center. I will never forget that. And as a reward, Kansas was the warm up band. They were awesome. But then Mick, Keith, Bill, Charley, and Ron took the stage and blew everyone's mind for two hours.

If they can enjoy their work that much, it must be possible for anyone else to do it too. Do what you do best, do what you enjoy, and don't hold back. Everyone loves to see someone on stage enjoying themselves and everyone has their own special talent. Find yours and go for it. That's what Mick on stage taught me and taught an entire generation. Get up on stage and go nuts. Why not? Of course first learn a skill, sing, play guitar, juggle, or dance, whatever it is. Then go nuts. Don't just go nuts doing something stupid.

The first time I saw the Rolling Stones was June 14th, 1978, at the Capitol Theater in Passaic, New Jersey. They were kicking off their tour after releasing their new album, 'Some Girls'. They wanted to start with a small theater, at the start of the tour, then on to more typically huge venues and stadiums.

My friend Mike and I drove out to New Jersey from Great Neck, Long Island where we were in high school. We didn't have tickets. We'd get in somehow, hopefully.

Outside the theater, Mike found a guy selling tickets for an astronomical sum. He didn't want to miss a possible opportunity but I decided to wait and see if I could get in for less money later. Mike had a little money to burn so why not? The guy sold him two tickets for a little over $300 (a ton of money at that time for a high school kid) and threw in a bag of 8 Quaaludes to sweeten the pot. Mike agreed. He'd try and resell the other ticket, and I would manage on my own. Or so we thought.

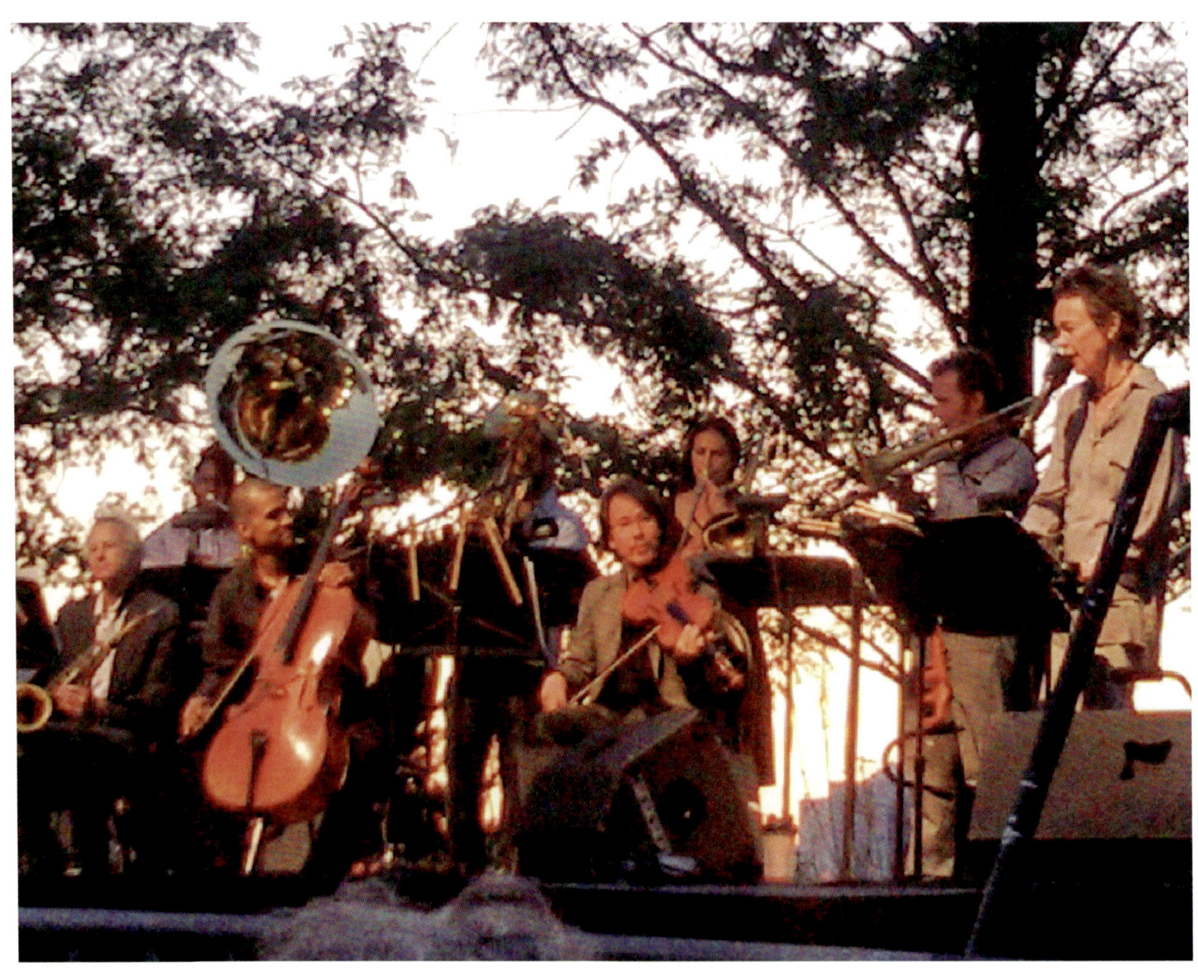

Laurie Anderson, June 2013

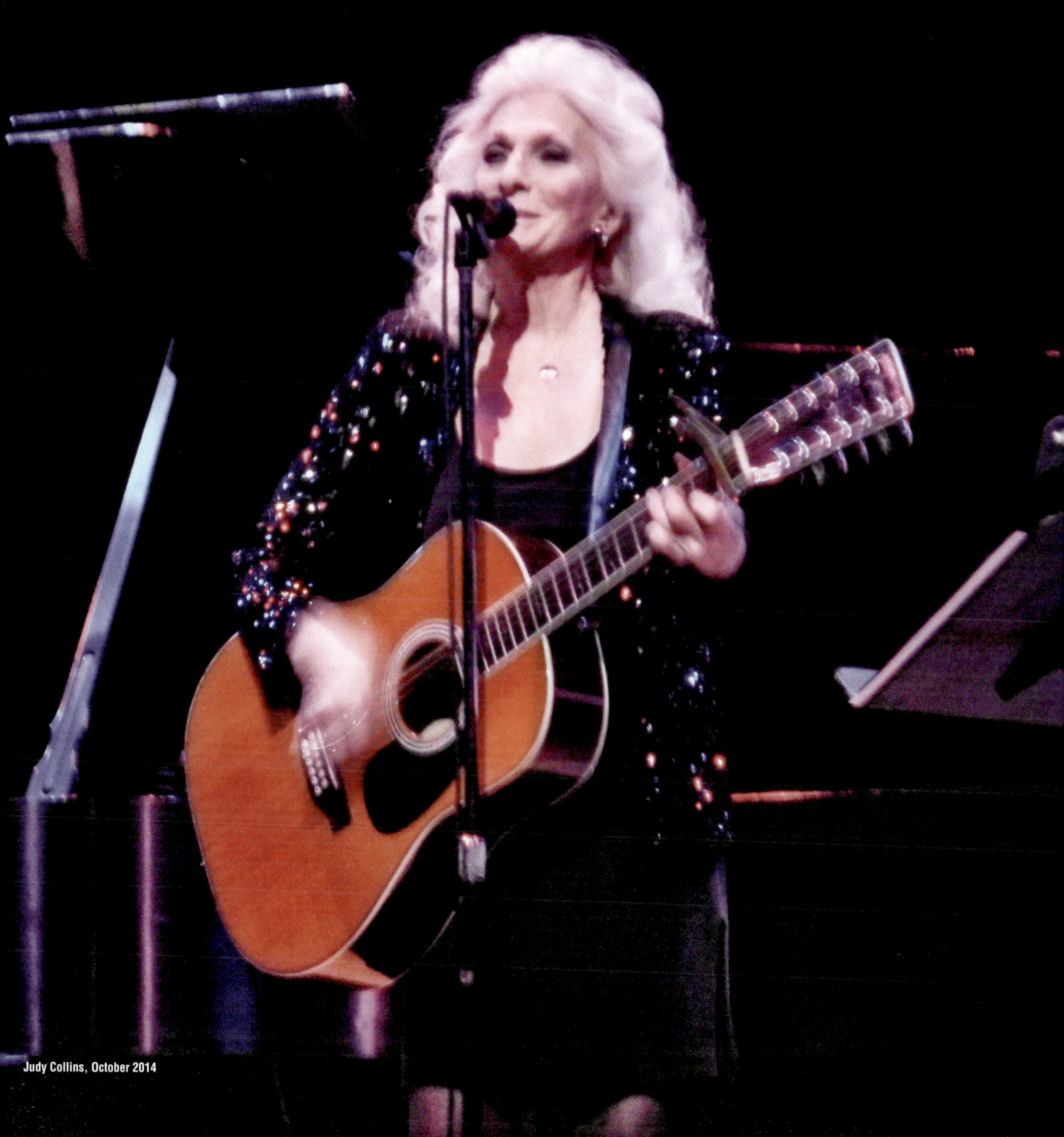

Judy Collins, October 2014

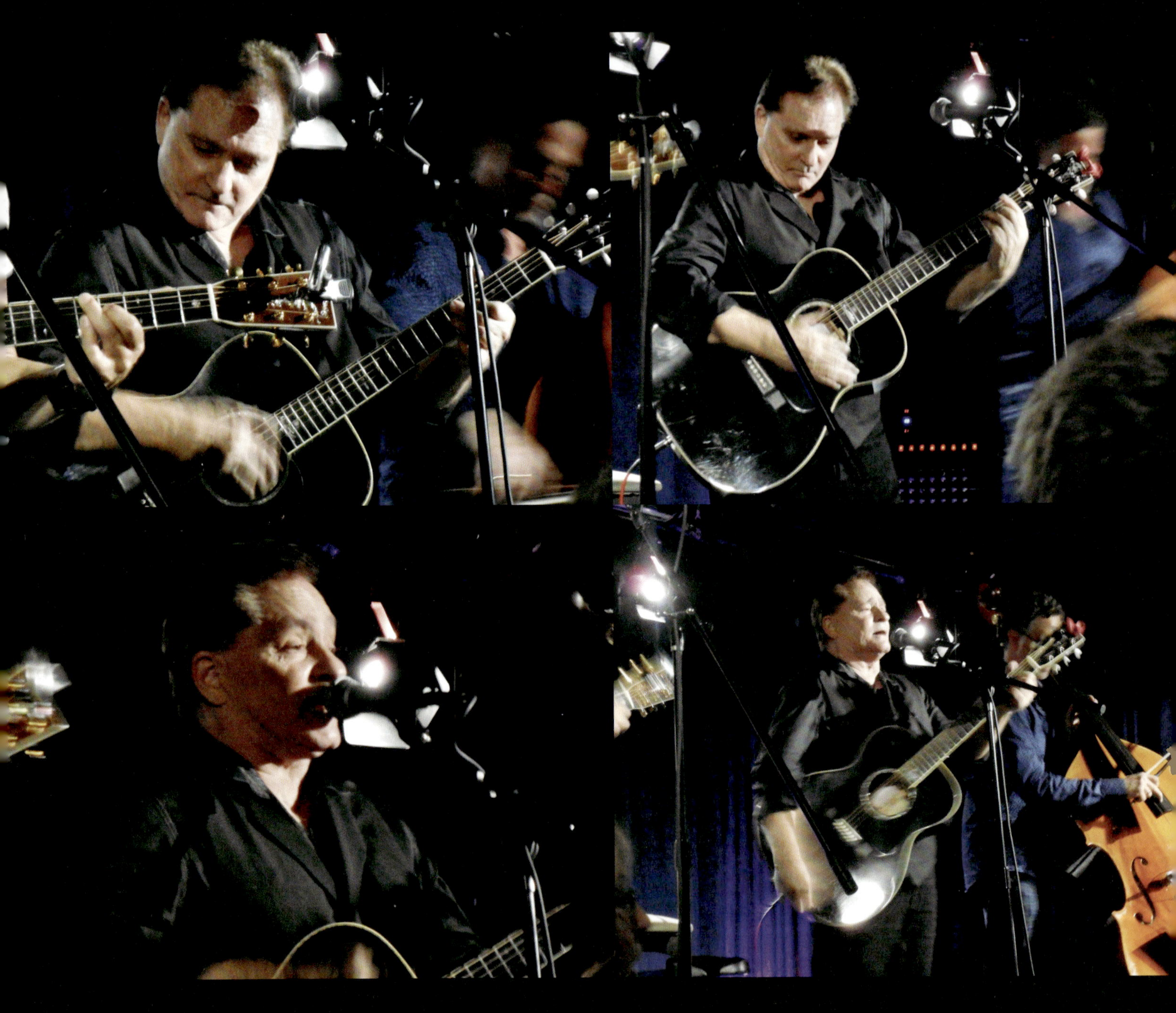

Marty Balin, October 2014

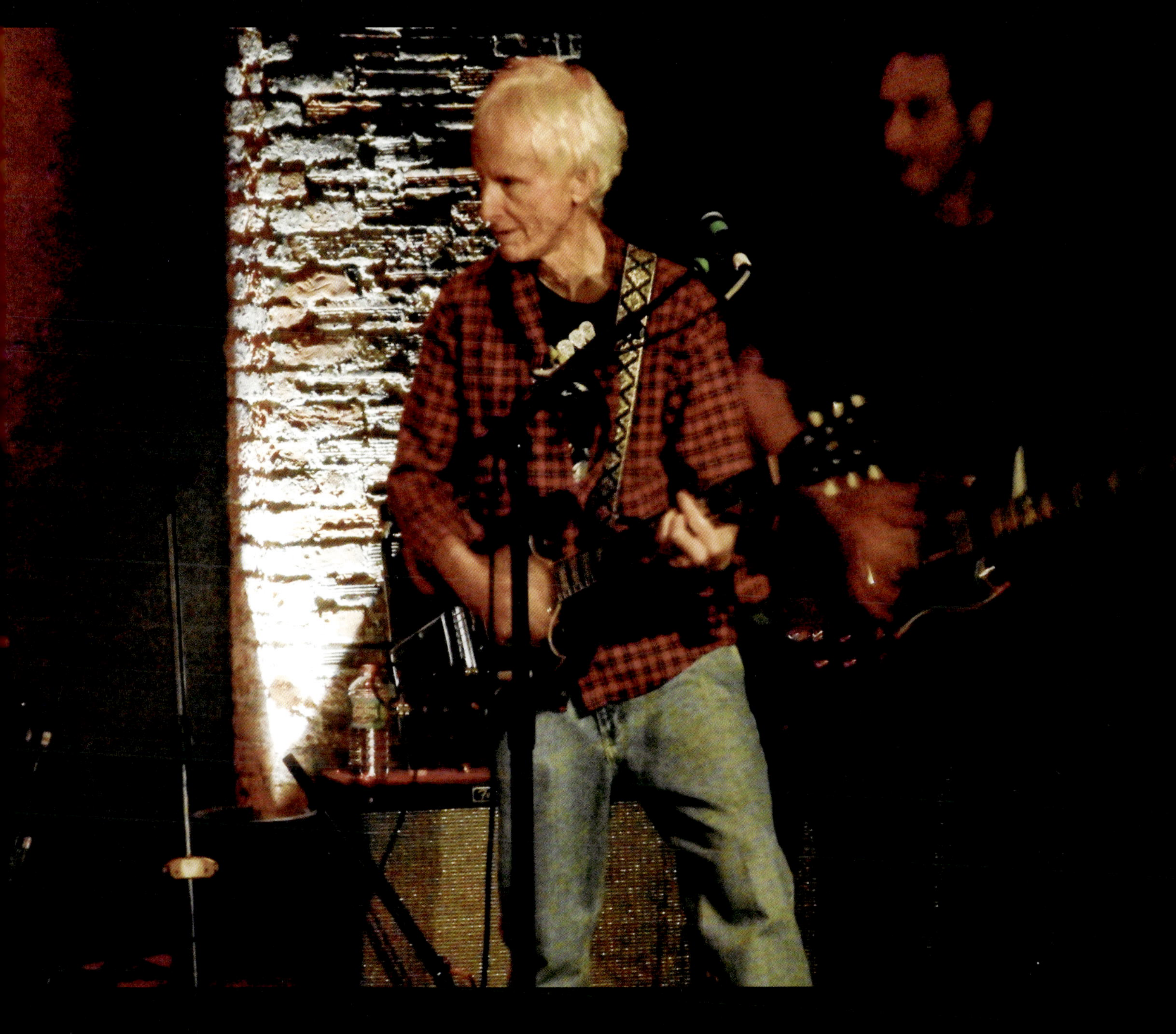

Robby Krieger (The Doors), April 2016

Once the price was agreed upon the question was where to make the switch.

"We're too close to the theater. Let's go off to the side where there are no people around and do it there," said the guy with the tickets and ludes.

"No, let's go over there by the corner where there is a big crowd of people around and do it there," said Mike. Neither could agree. Finally:

"Okay, let's just do it here".

"Here are the tickets and Quaaludes, thank you." "Okay here is the money."

"Stop! You're under arrest!"

The cops grabbed Mike and the other guy and arrested them, presumably for scalping tickets. As they were taking Mike away in the Paddy Wagon, he told one of the cops to reach into his pocket please and give me one of the tickets (his own hands were cuffed at the time). The cop did it and next think I know I'm in the tenth row, sitting a few seats away from Billy Joel in the audience, and hearing Mick belt out "Miss You" and "Street Fighting Man". I'll never forget that. Neither will Mike whose father bailed him out and arranged for his lawyer to have the charges (he was charged with selling Quaaludes which didn't even make sense) all dropped.

Other groups supplemented their music with some kind of 'light-show'. But the Stones were themselves the light show. Still, some very clever and entertaining light-shows were created. Jefferson Starship always had some kind of psychedelic visuals going on to keep you mellow if you were on too many substances. I remember the entire venue bathed in yellow light and then red spotlights going in all directions all over the stage, audience, and ceiling. Very trippy. That was in the Nassau Coliseum in 1977. The same year The Who in Madison Square Garden were experimenting with laser lights. Very innovative. This can be seen in the movie, "The Kids Are Alright".

The term "Rock Concert" can actually take a very wide variety of forms, both musically and visually. In 1979 I saw Jorma Kaukonen play a solo concert. Just Jorma and a guitar. Jorma- the magnificent guitarist for Jefferson Airplane and Hot Tuna. Jefferson Airplane broke up into Jefferson Starship and Hot Tuna, and Hot Tuna eventually broke up and got back together later. So I caught Jorma right in the middle of all that when he was solo and it was dynamite. He played "Embryonic Journey" from the Airplane days and "Mann's Fate" from the Hot Tuna days, and many others. You have to call that a rock concert, he's the guitarist for two of the most important rock bands of the century.

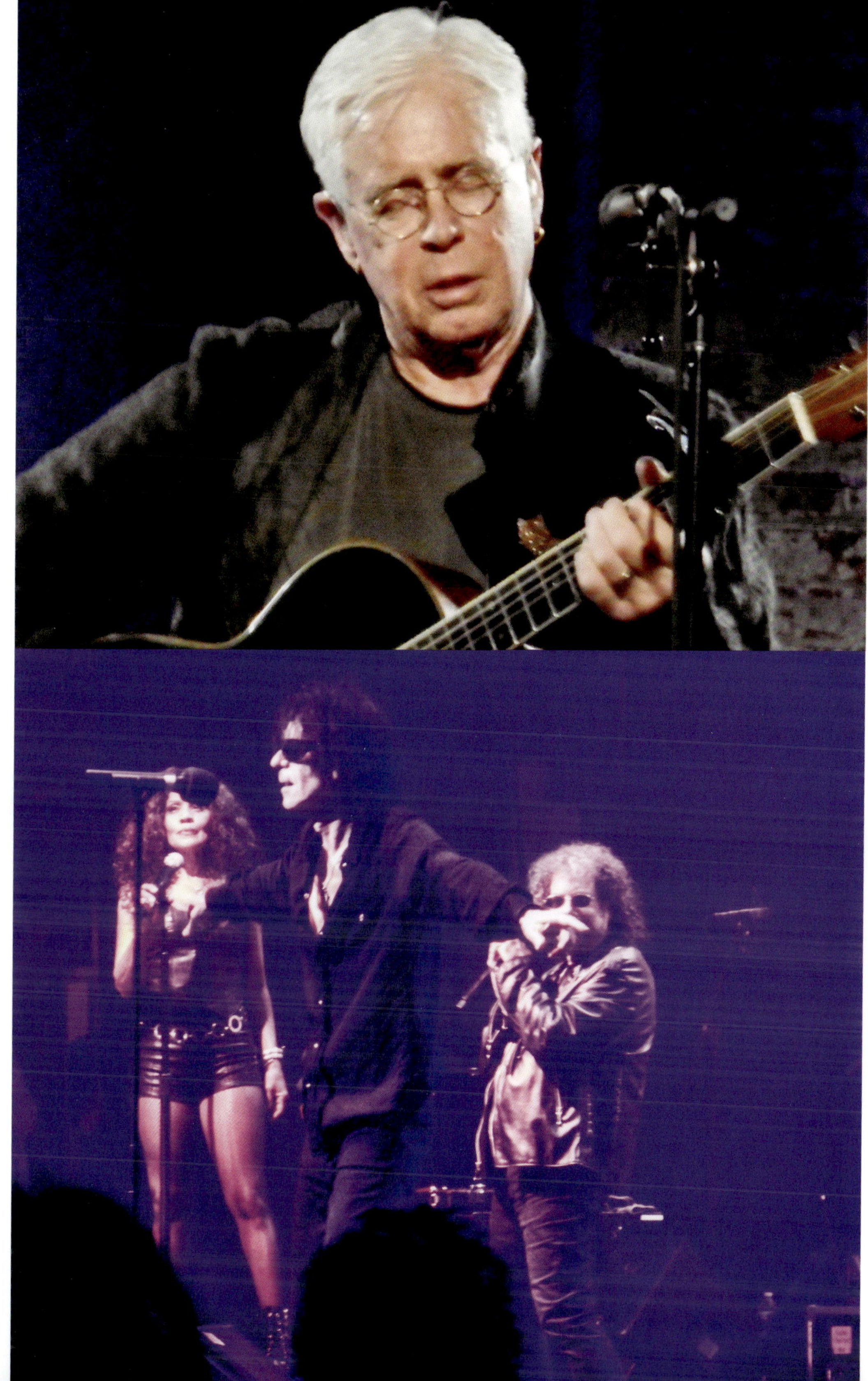

Bruce Cockburn, November 2014

J. Geils Band, August 2015

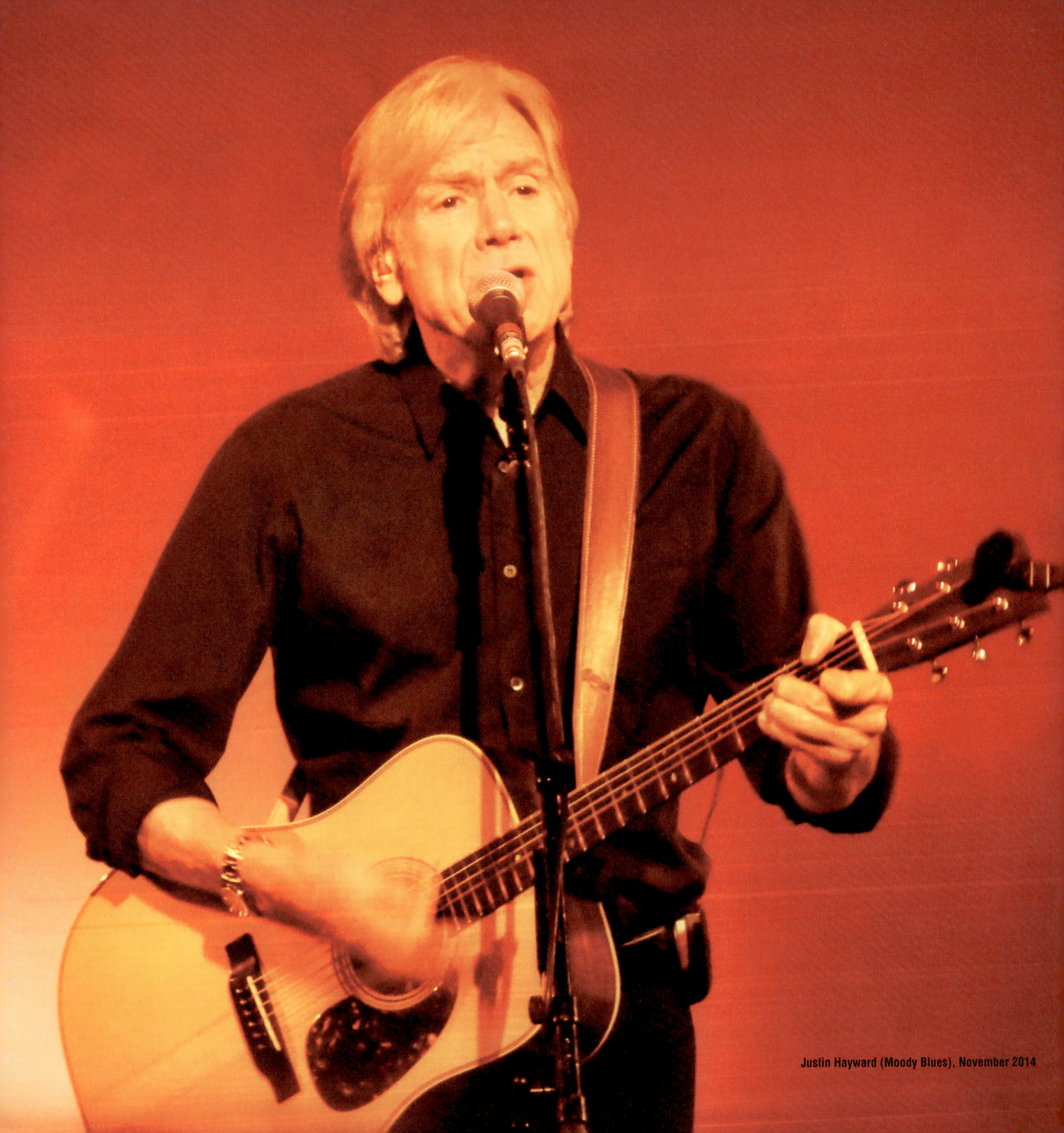

Justin Hayward (Moody Blues), November 2014

Contrary-wise, I recently saw Kiss play a concert. Exactly the opposite. Tons of effects, pyrotechnics, flame throwing, flame spitting, flame shooting, costumes, make-up, and machinery. Okay, very entertaining but what about the music? Well, yes there was some music there too. But the music is an excuse to throw flames and dress up. You can't just go on stage and dress up and throw flames. It has to be in some sort of context. Still, Kiss have sold over a hundred million albums, believe it or not, so someone must enjoy their music on its own. I'm not putting Kiss down. They are artists and expressing themselves artistically, and doing an entertaining job of it. And they have many original ideas and have been copied from the earth to the sky and all over. They may not be demonstrating against the war in Vietnam, or protesting against the spread of Sharia law, but they are giving us something to fight for. Freedom of expression and the right to the pursuit of happiness.

If I had any criticism for Kiss it would be fairer to compare them to Alice Cooper. Alice also has effects, and fake blood, and pyrotechnics, and theatrics and make-up. But Alice never takes himself too seriously. He's always doing his ridiculous stunts with a sort of tongue–in-cheek attitude. This is all very scary and tough so watch it and enjoy it but keep in mind on the back burner that this is all a joke. Kiss on the other hand shoot fire and spit blood, but they seem actually to mean it.

 In 1972 my friend Glen went to an Alice Cooper concert. He was only twelve. His older teenage cousins were out the door to the concert when Glen's mother asked them what they were doing. When they told her they were going to see Alice Cooper she told them to bring Glen along. So these cool teenagers had to drag this little kid along and when they got there Alice gets tied up by zombie nurses and thrown into a guillotine and gets his head chopped off, and the poor kid was terrified and had to leave the theater and wait in the lobby sobbing for two hours until the cousins came out and brought him home.

The only time I was ever scared at a concert was in 1979 when I went with my pal Jimmy to see The Outlaws, Todd Rundgren, and Boston, in Giants Stadium, Meadowland, New Jersey, June 17th. We actually went to see The Outlaws but I became a huge fan of Todd and Boston after seeing them live. At the end of the show, the finale was Boston doing their encore. In the middle of their finale the musicians step back and for a split second the stage is empty. Suddenly an explosion erupts with an earth shattering BOOM and a wall of fire fills the stage. The wall of fire disappears, the musicians return and the song is finished. But for anyone in the first ten rows (and of course we were in the first row, it's general admission, after all, no fixed seating, no seats at all on the floor) the explosion lives on in your mind which is shattered, eyes full of after-burn, ears ringing and eye-brows singed. Giants Stadium has a capacity of over eighty thousand people. That effect was designed to be seen by people as far as a block away. We were about ten feet away. That was a moment of extreme clarity.

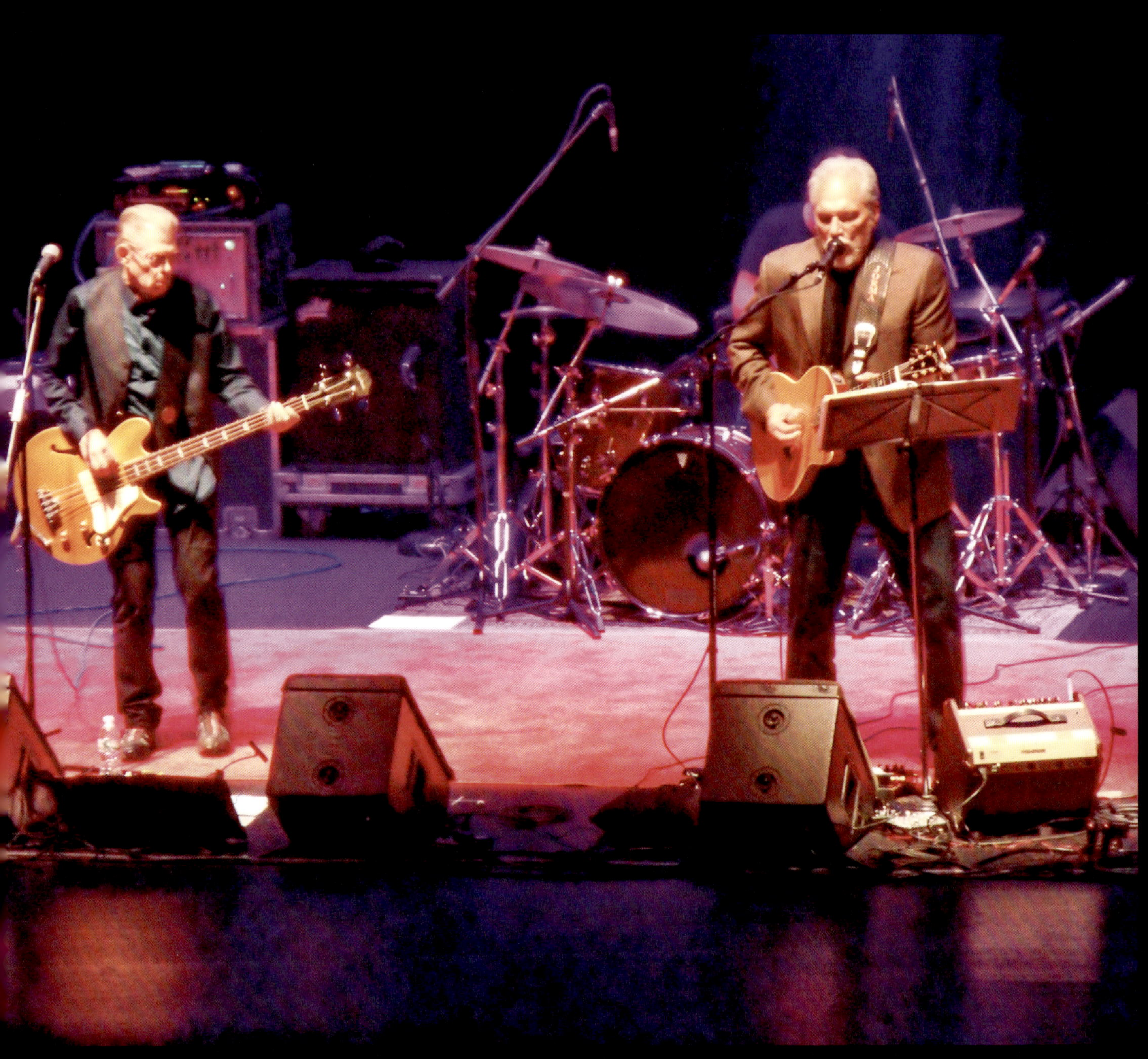

Hot Tuna, November 2015

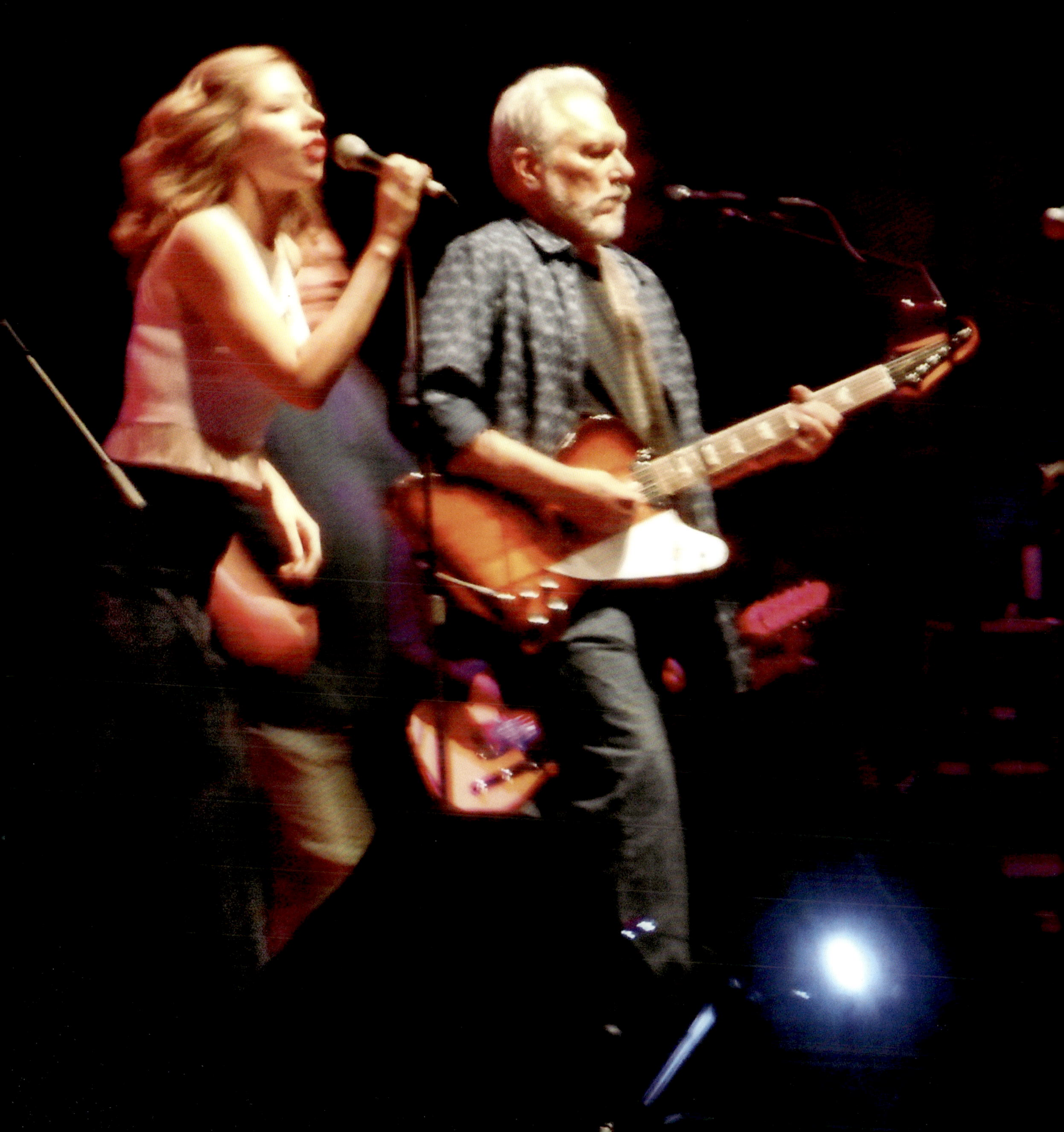

Many concerts in New York are free. Some take place in Central Park. And speaking of free concerts in Central Park and pushing (politely) to the front, I notice a dangerous trend these days. I saw several free concerts in Central Park in the 70s. Jefferson Starship, The Beach Boys, and Elton John. If you got there early enough and you had the tenacity you could push (politely) to the front. I remember them saying there were 400,000 people at Elton John. He changed costumes three times including a giant Donald Duck outfit.

Unfortunately in the last few years, the big free concerts in Central Park (Neil Young and Foo Fighters in 2012, and Stevie Wonder and Alisha Keys in 2013 for example) have been organized so that you can't do that anymore and it stinks. Once a section or 'pen' is full, it is closed and the next section is opened. So you can only push to the front of your 'pen'. What a rip off! Then they justify it by putting up huge screens so you can see the stage from a mile away. But it's like watching TV! Excuse me but I want to see Neil Young up close, not a block away with binoculars (I refuse to even look at the screen). It's 1984.

They don't do that at the smaller concerts-yet.

Now let's talk about the Grateful Dead but first let's talk about the Beatles.

The Beatles were touring extensively in the early 60s but pretty much stopped after President Ferdinand Marcus kicked them out of the Philippines! The Beatles had been performing relentlessly for years, and were on a world tour in 1966 after recording the album Revolver. The First Lady, Imelda Marcus invited them to an official state breakfast where she'd hoped they could meet their teenage daughters who were huge Beatle fans. The Beatles were exhausted and had to fly out early the next day and politely declined.

In Asia it is an insult to refuse a gift or an invitation. News of this grave crime was published in the papers and the whole country went nuts. The police refused to escort them to the airport. They had to get there on their own. Asian peoples feel their leaders are divinely appointed through karma or reincarnation. So to insult an Asian king or president is like insulting the Buddha. They barely escaped a riot and were almost lynched. Their road manager Mal Evans was beaten to a pulp, the band was jostled, pushed, and had things thrown at them and Brian Epstein had to pay a ransom of 68,000 pounds sterling (a colossal sum in those days) in 'tax' to be allowed to leave.

When later asked if they would ever return to the Philippines, John Lennon said, 'only with an H-bomb.' Shortly after this, the Beatles stopped touring. Later that same year ('66) John was again the center of controversy when newspapers reported that he had publicly said, "The Beatles are better than Jesus" or "More Big than God" or other misquotes. What he had actually said was, "The Beatles are bigger than Jesus", which is no big deal. So people started buying their records to burn them and he came on TV and apologized and explained that he was actually criticizing society by saying that, what kind of world are we living in where young people are more concerned with

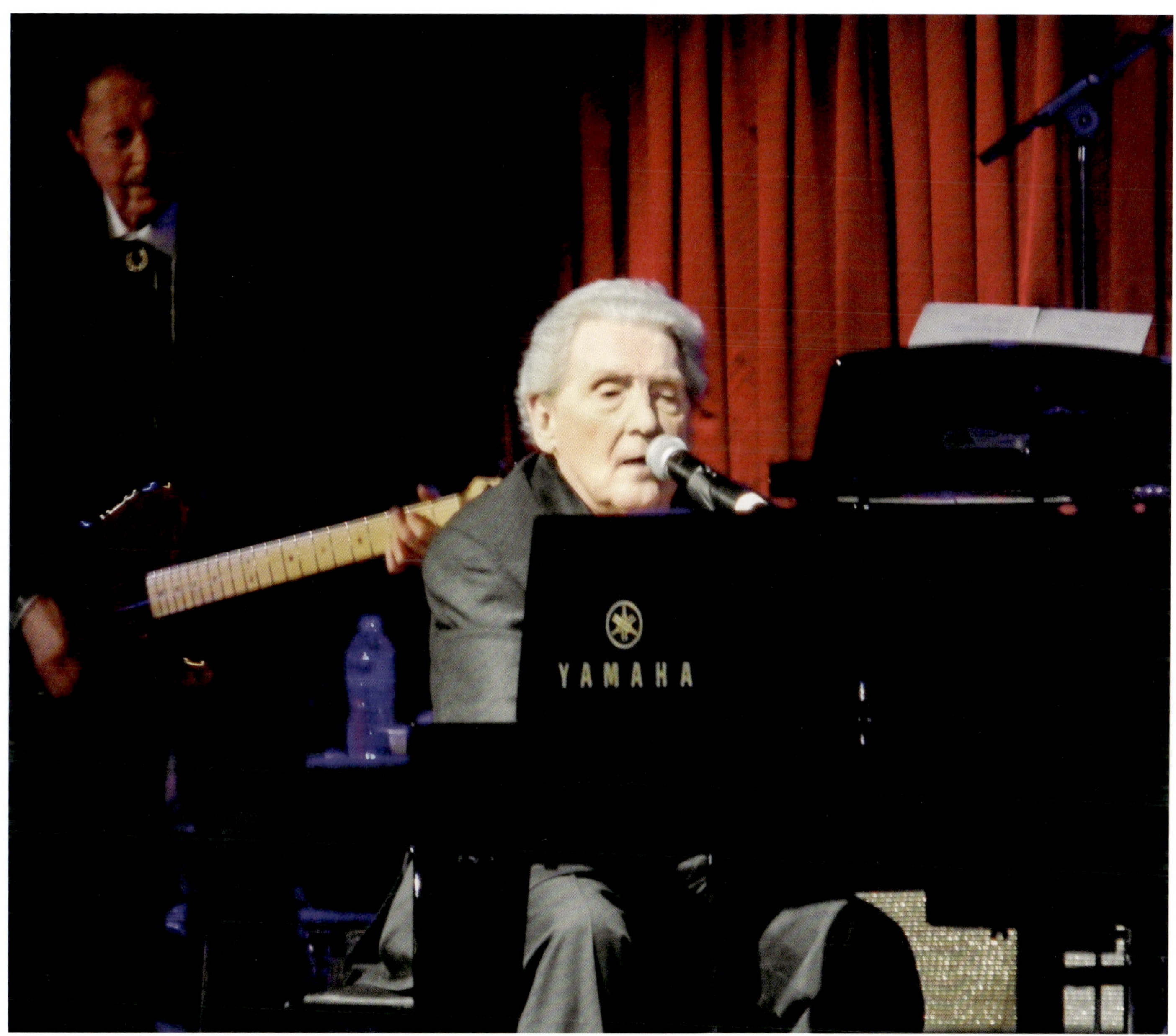

Jerry Lee Lewis, December 2015

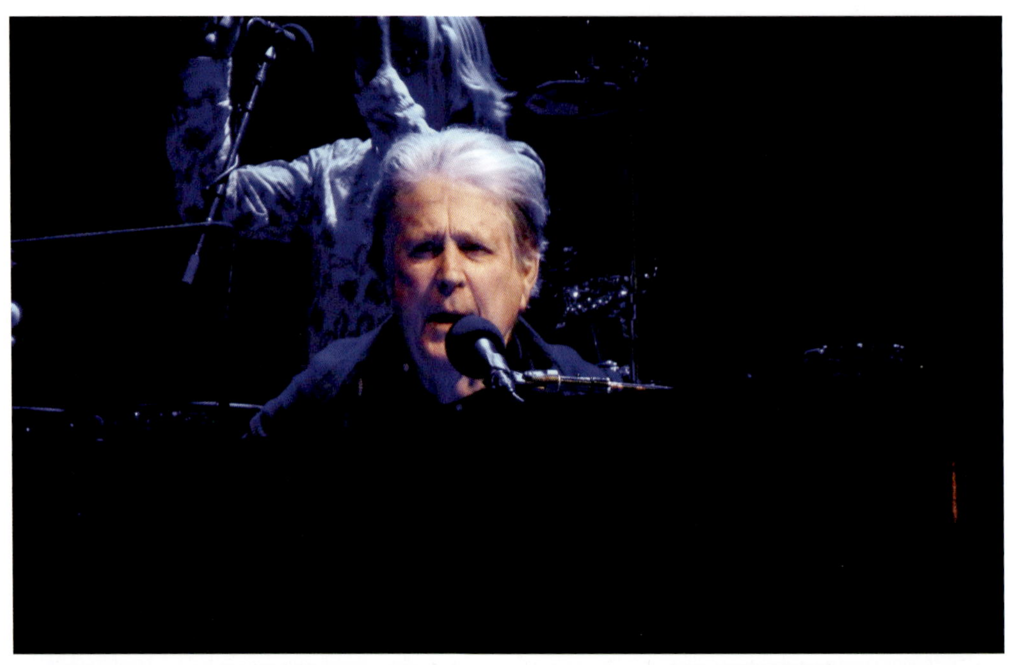

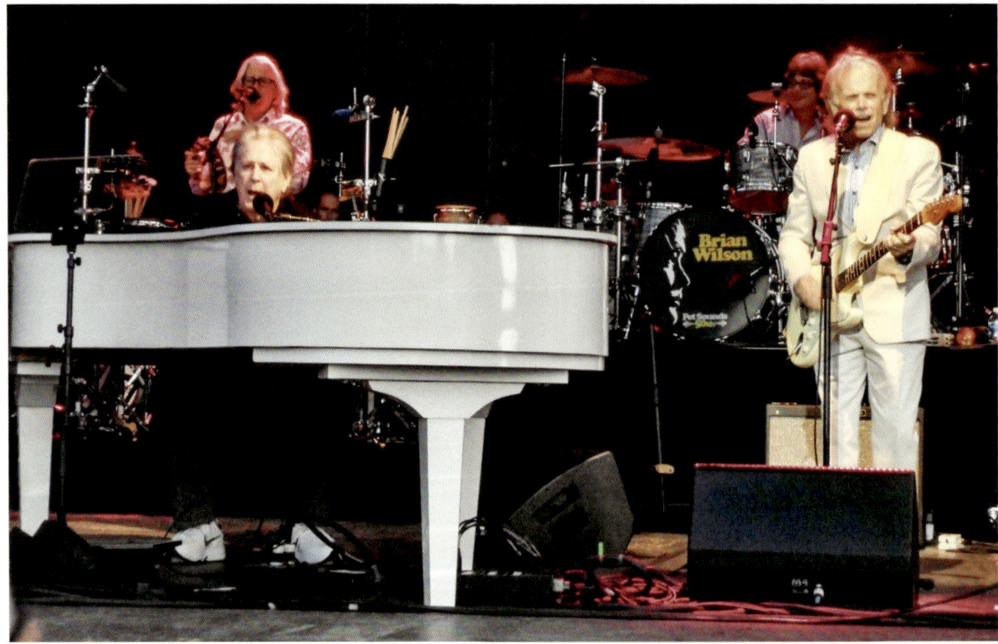

Brian Wilson, June 2016
Brian Wilson and Al Jardin (The Beach Boys), June 2016

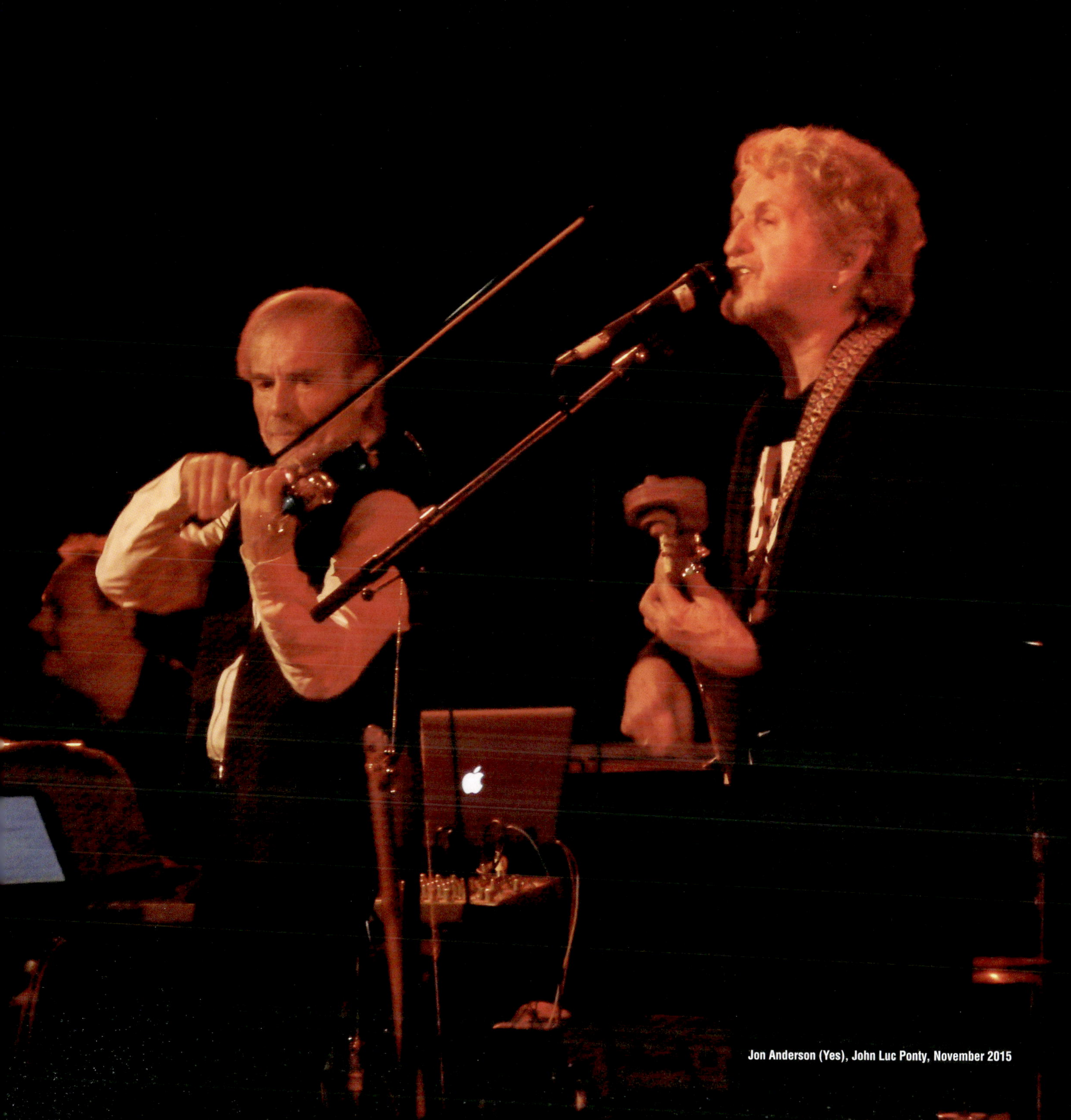

Jon Anderson (Yes), John Luc Ponty, November 2015

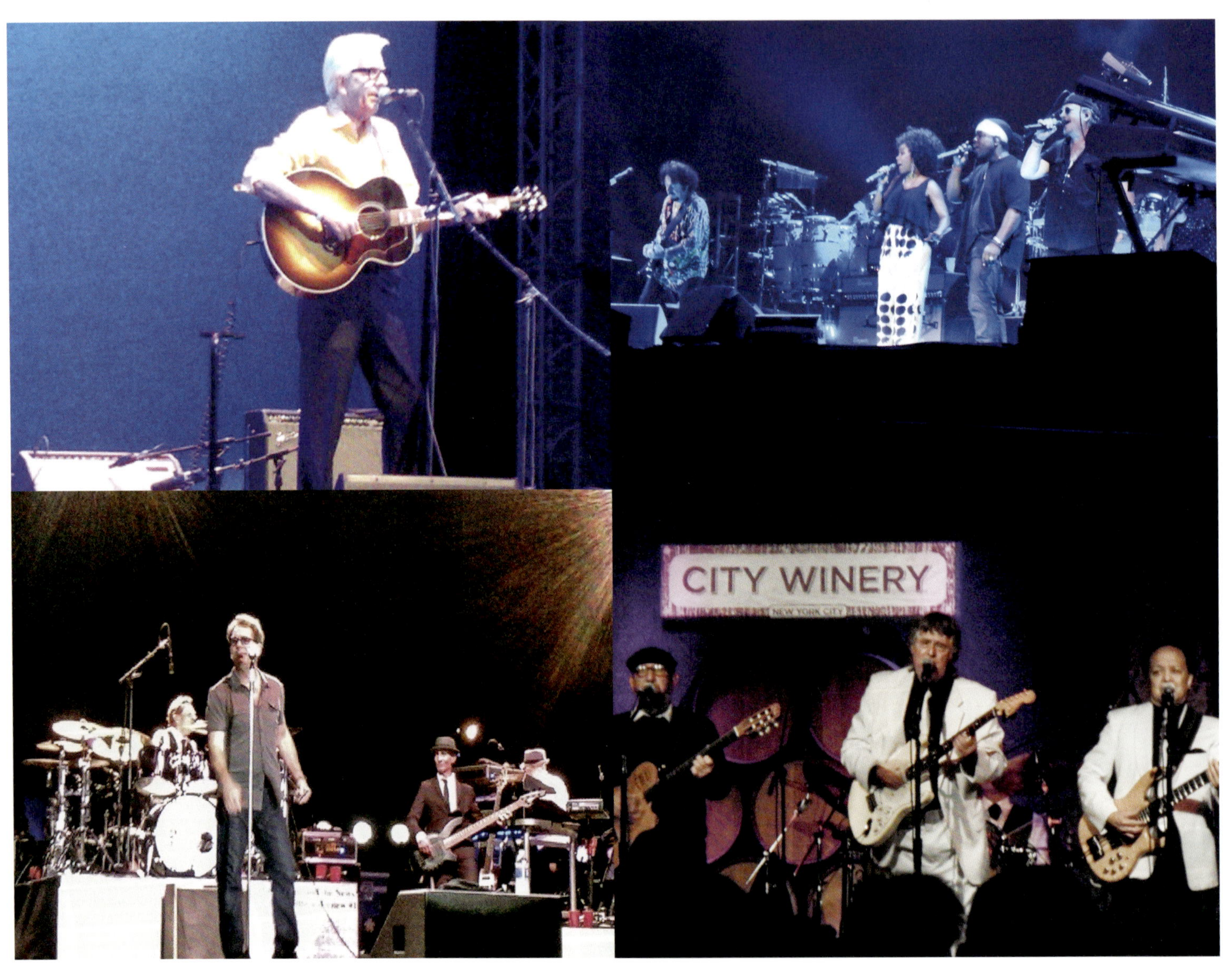

Nick Lowe (Rock  Pile), August 2013

Toto, August 2014

Huey Lewis and the News, August 2013

The Association, November 2014

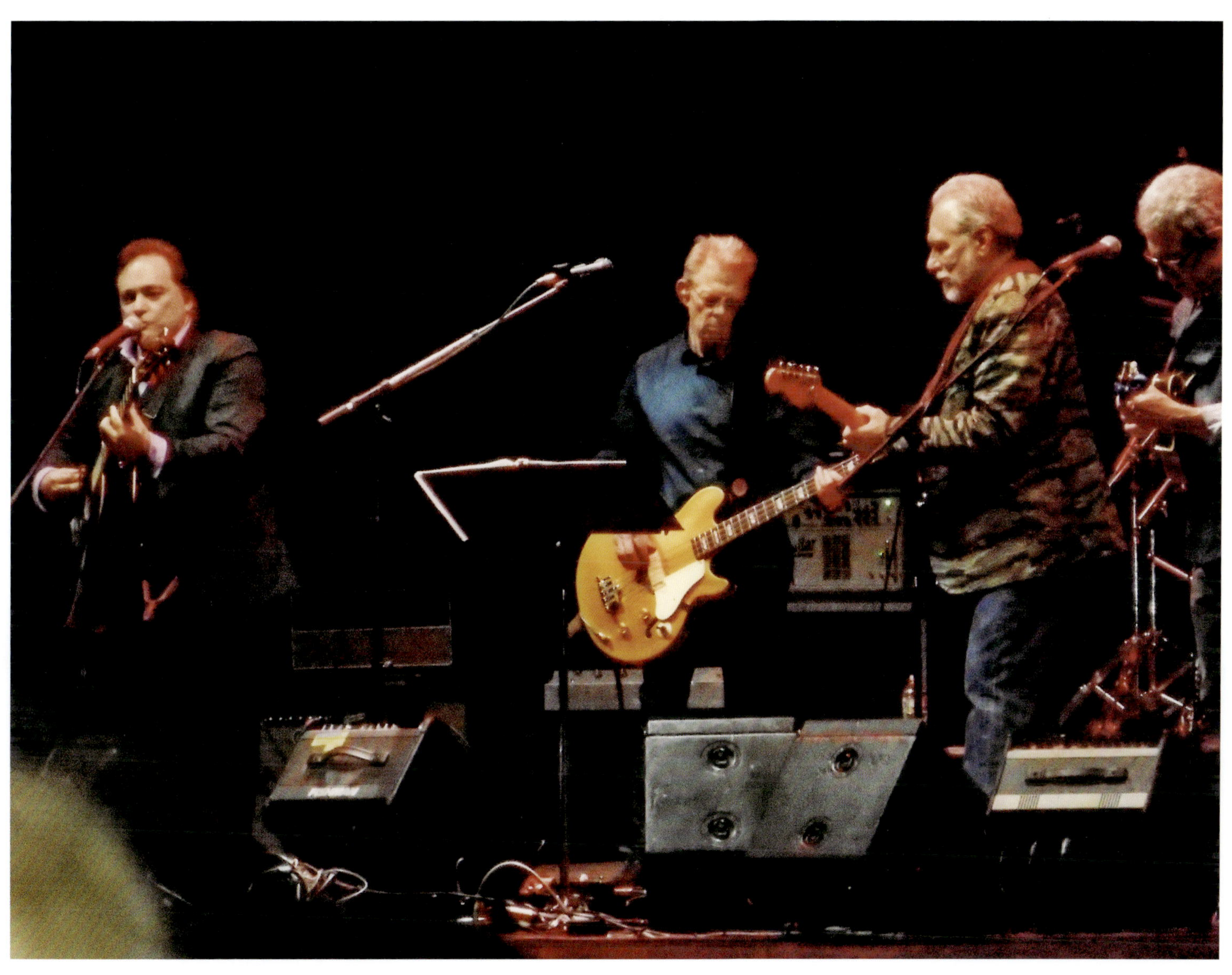

Jefferson Airplane (from left-Marty Balin,Jefferson Airplane,
Jefferson Starship; Jack Cassidy-Jefferson Airplane, Hot Tuna;
Jorma Kaukonen-Jefferson Airplane, Hot Tuna), December 2014

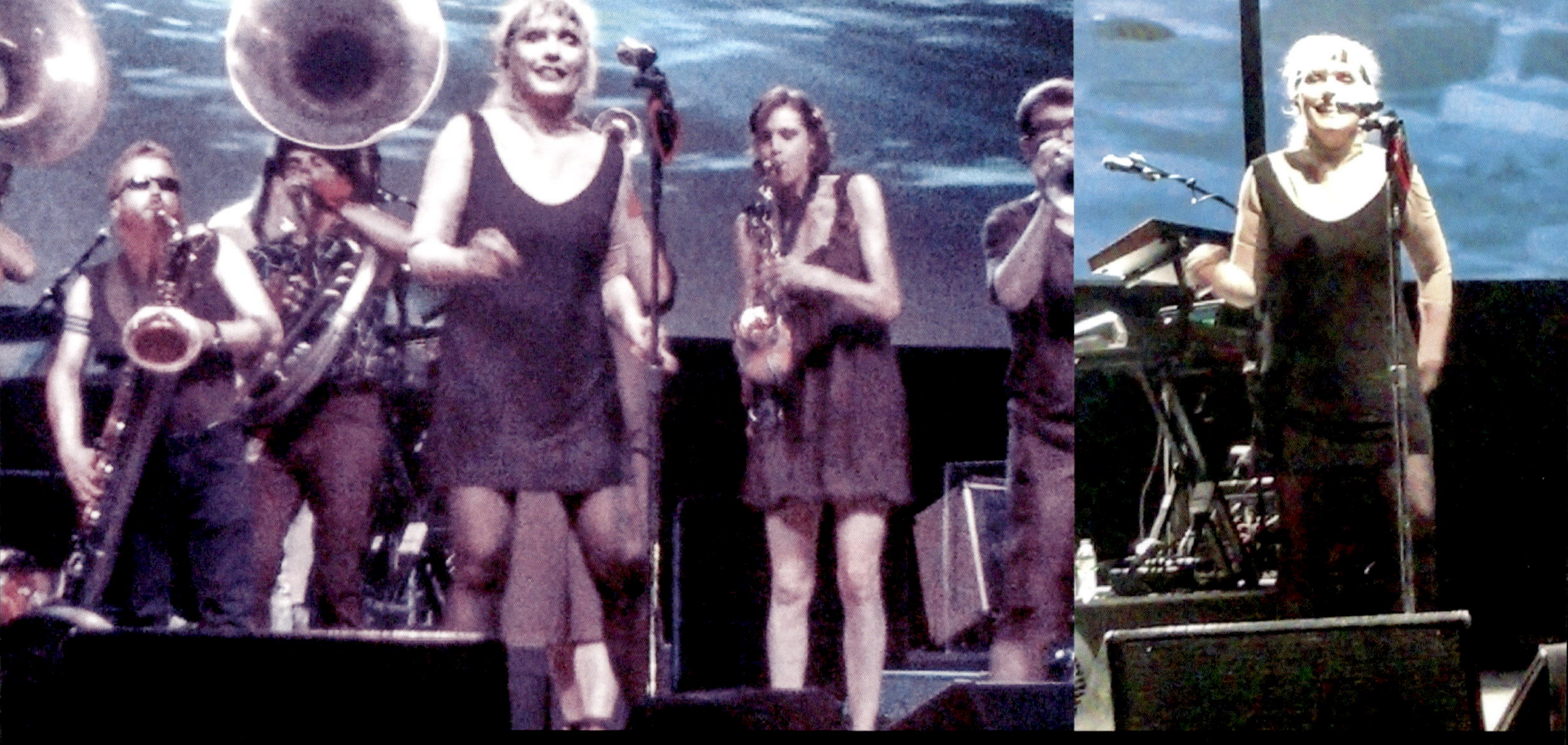

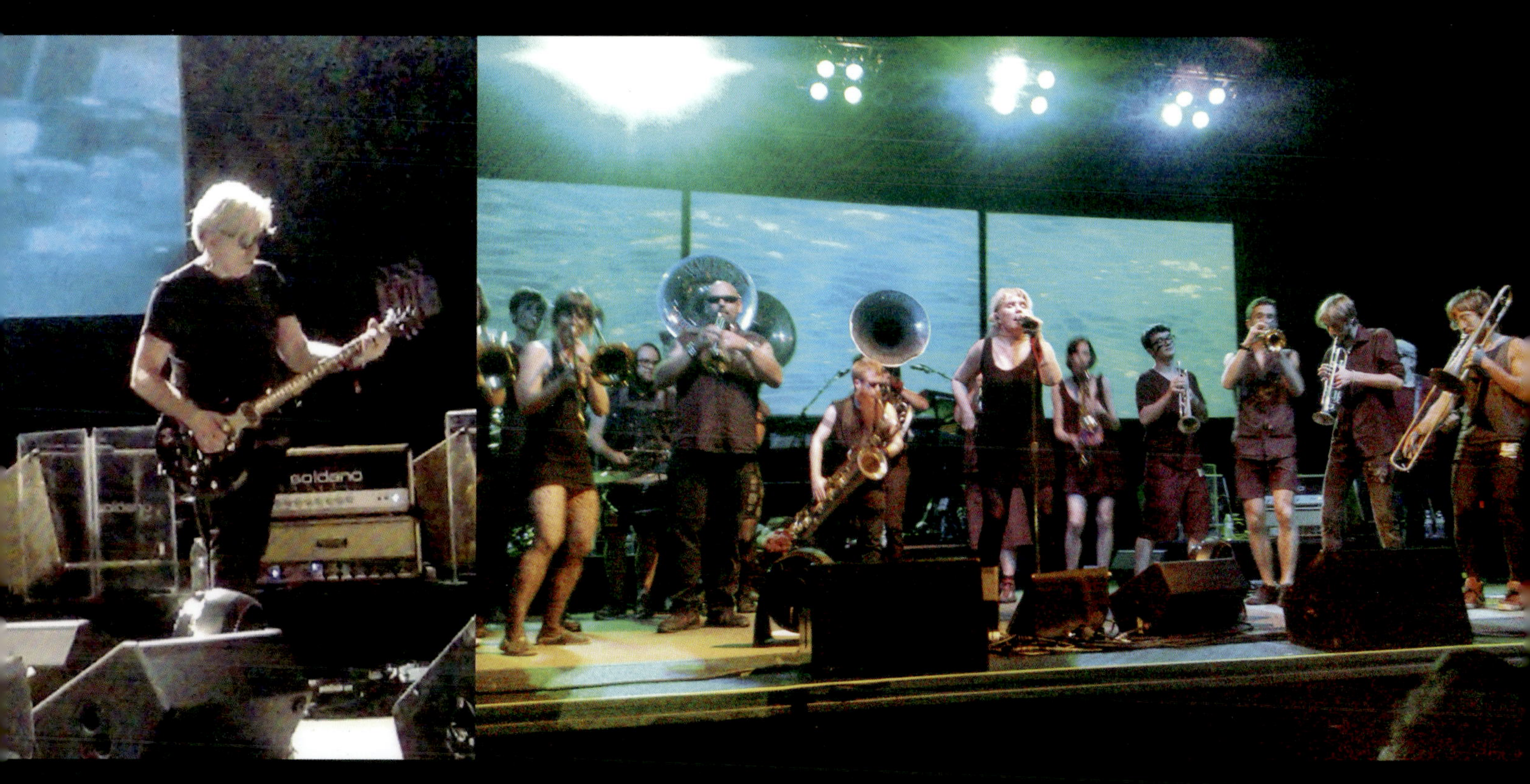

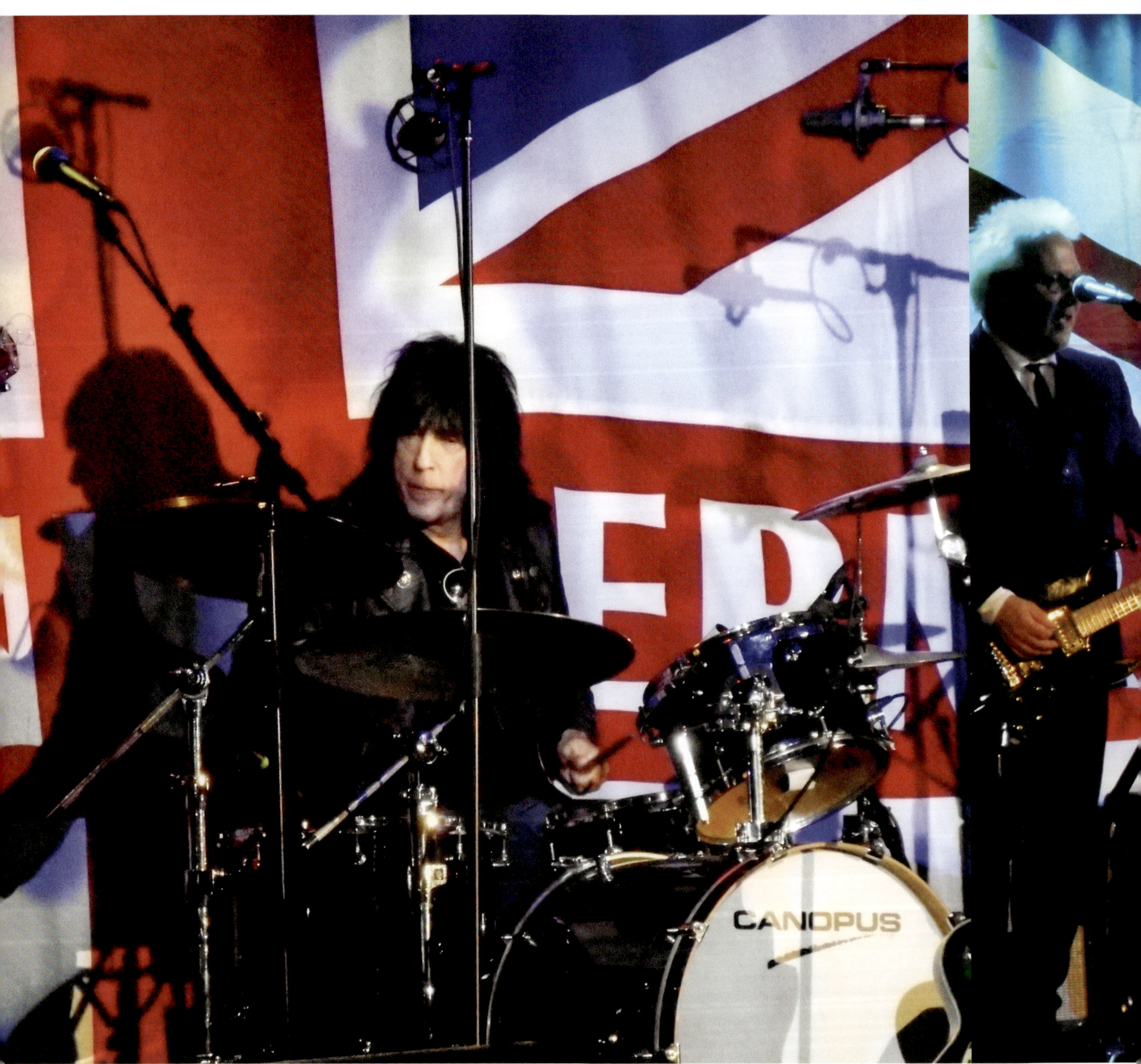



**Marky Ramone (The Ramones), November 2015**

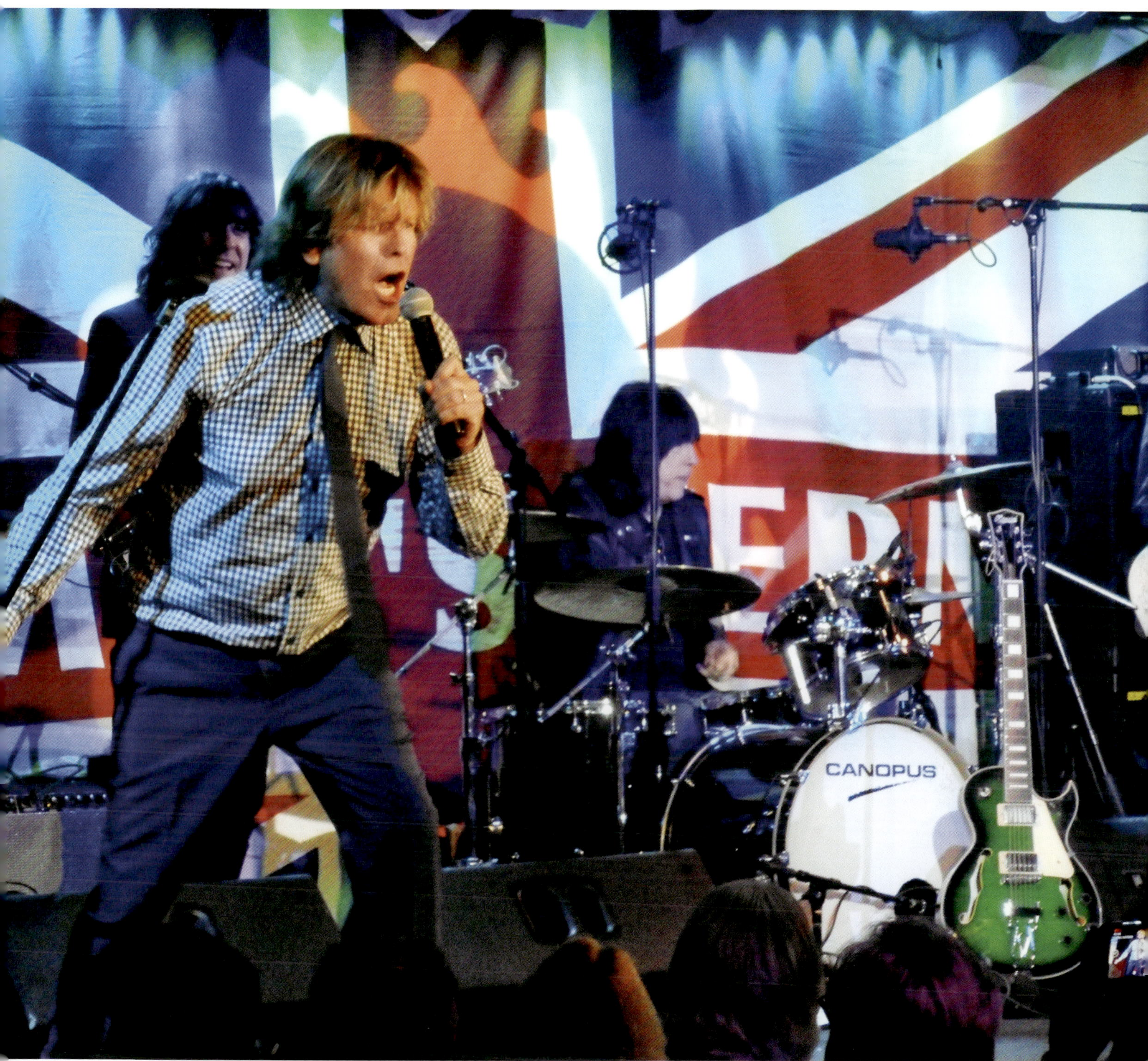

Herman's Hermits with guest drummer, Marky Ramone, November 2015

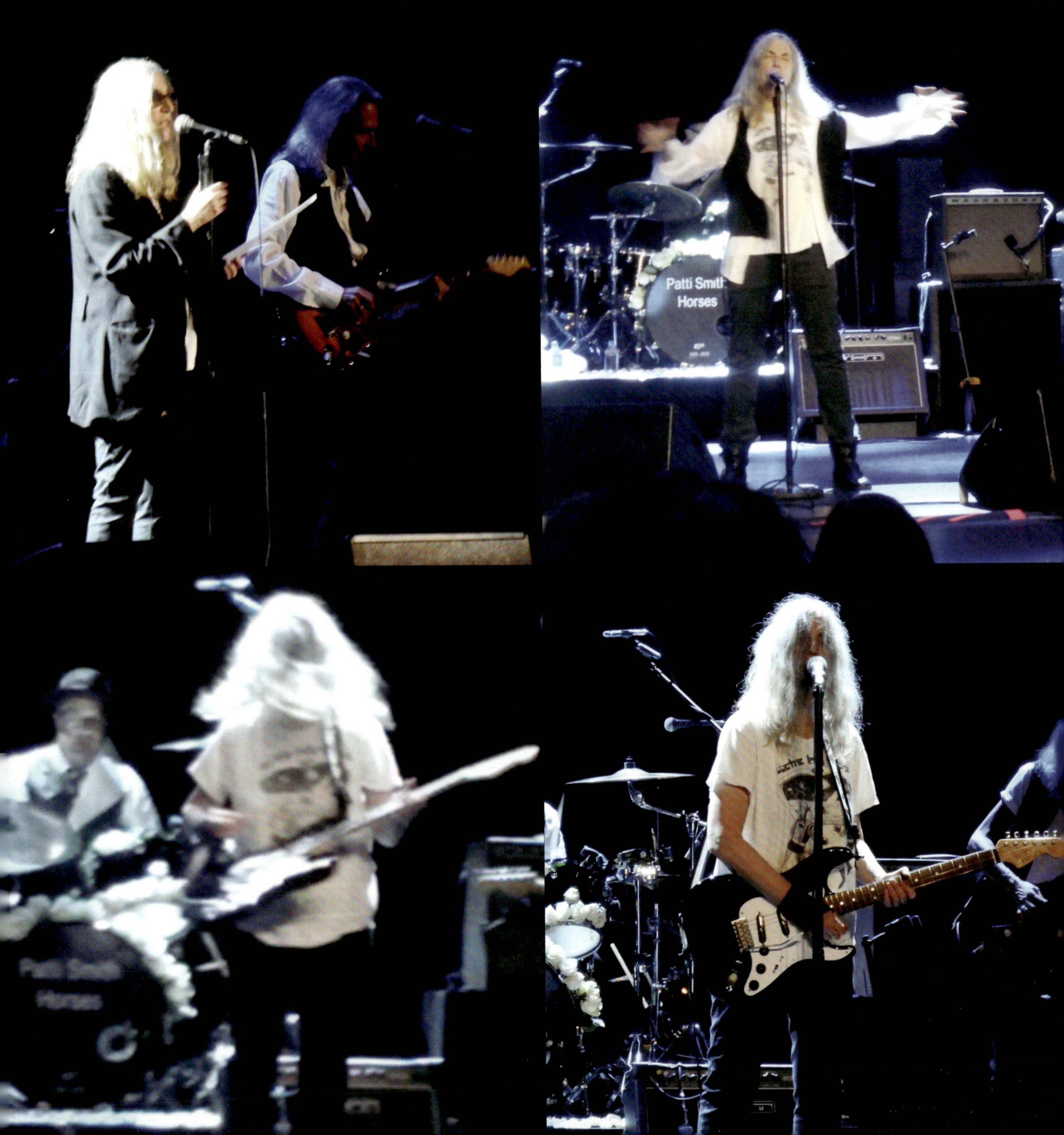

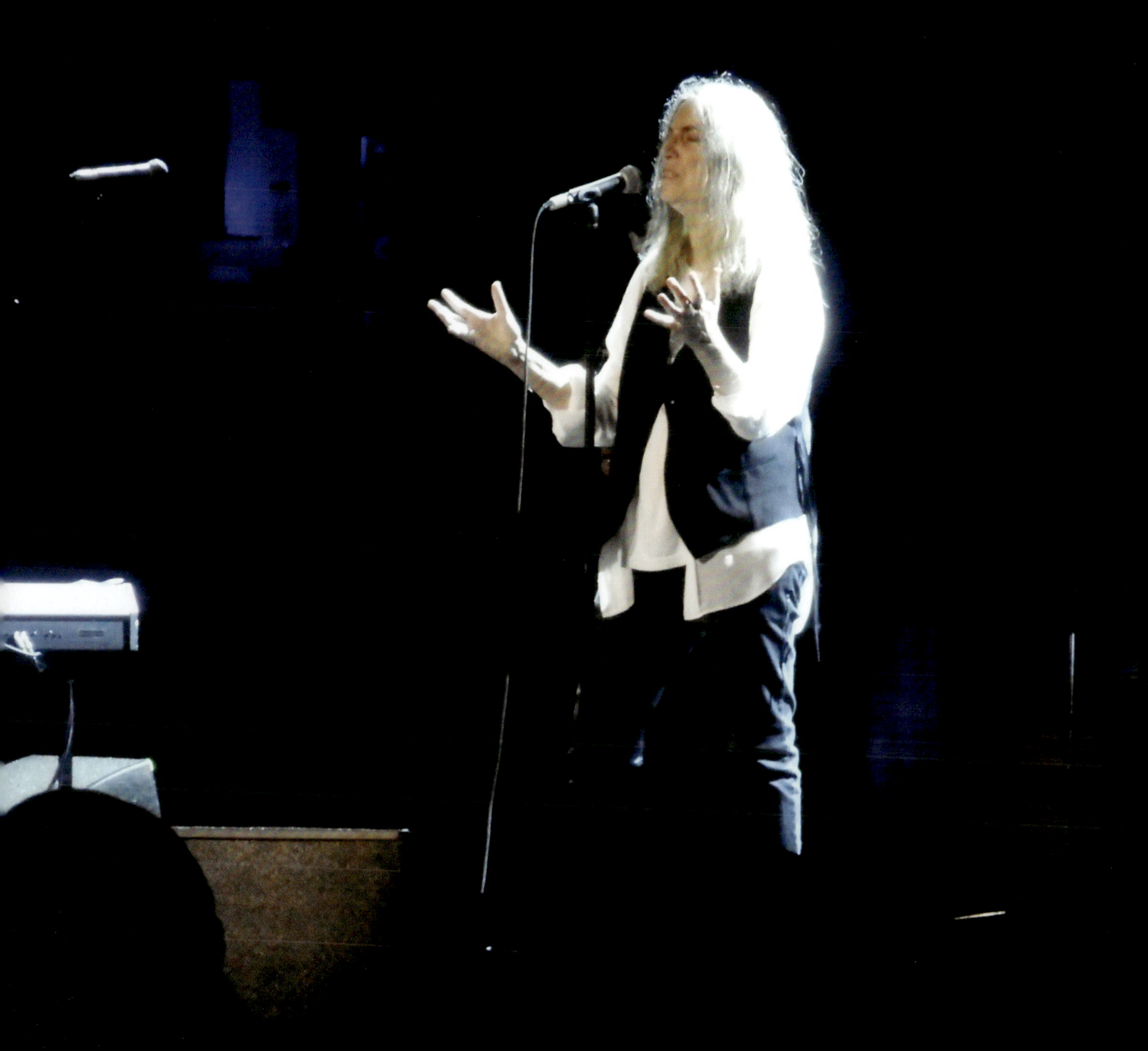

Patti Smith, November 2015

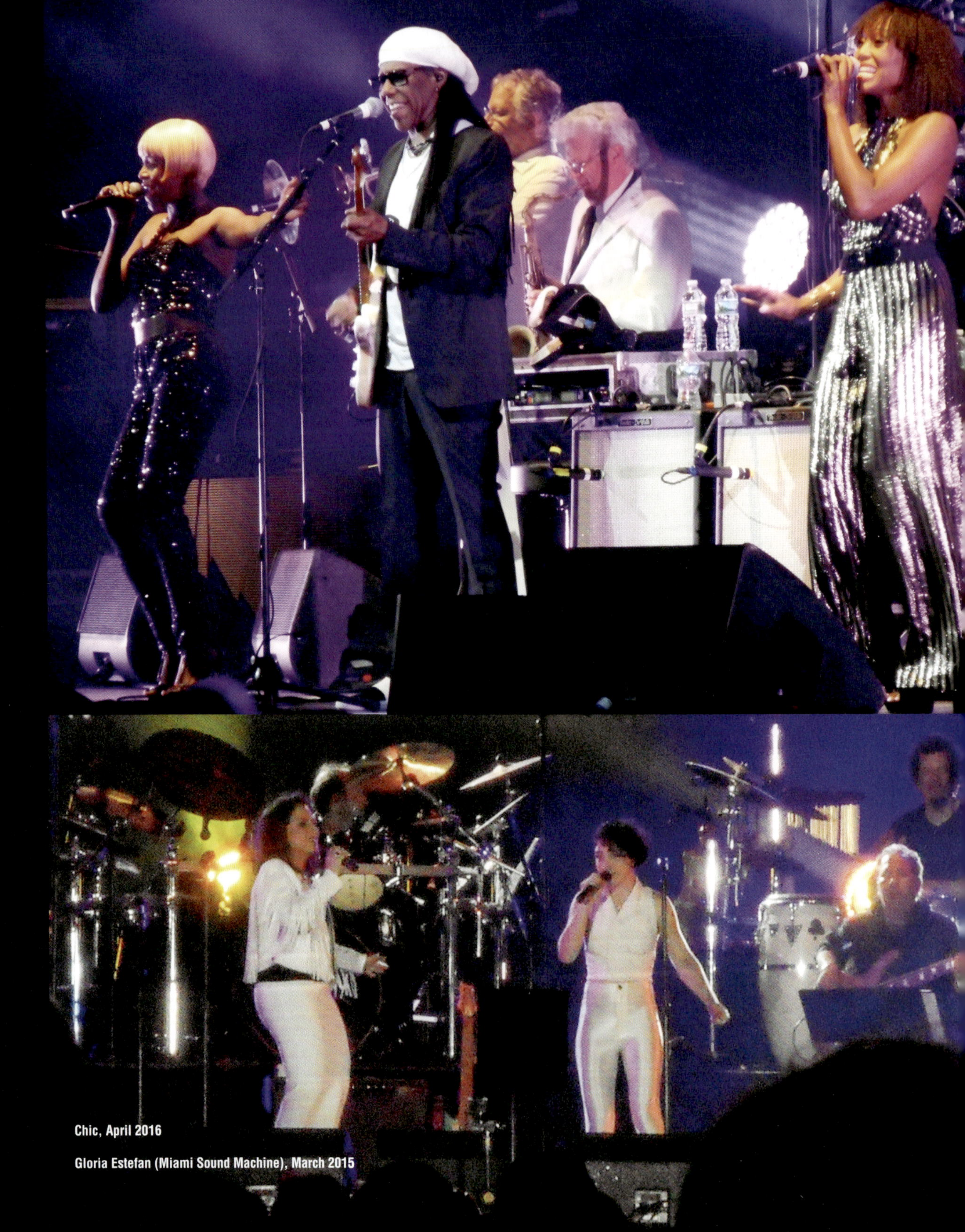

Chic, April 2016

Gloria Estefan (Miami Sound Machine), March 2015

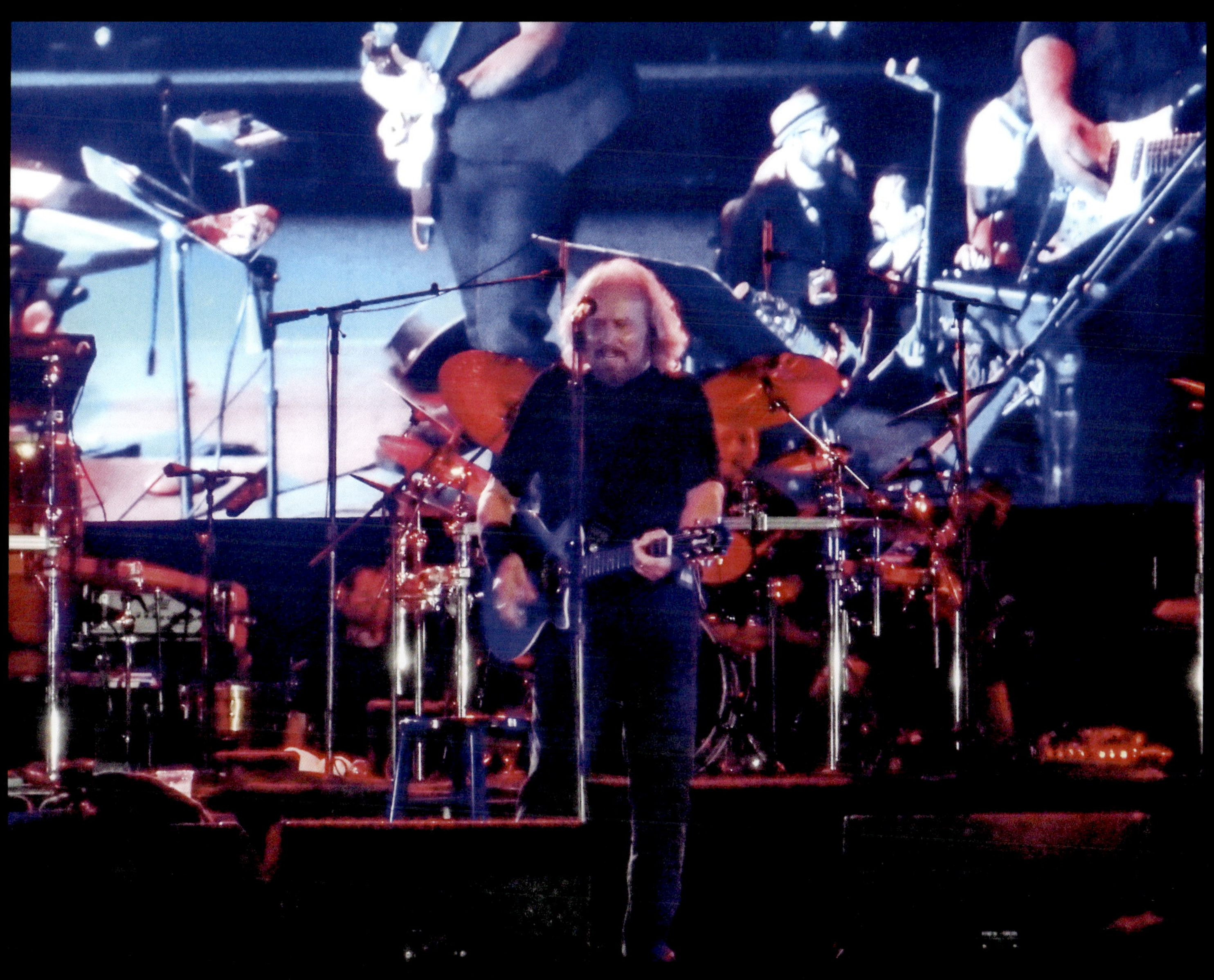

Barry Gibb (Bee Gees), March 2015

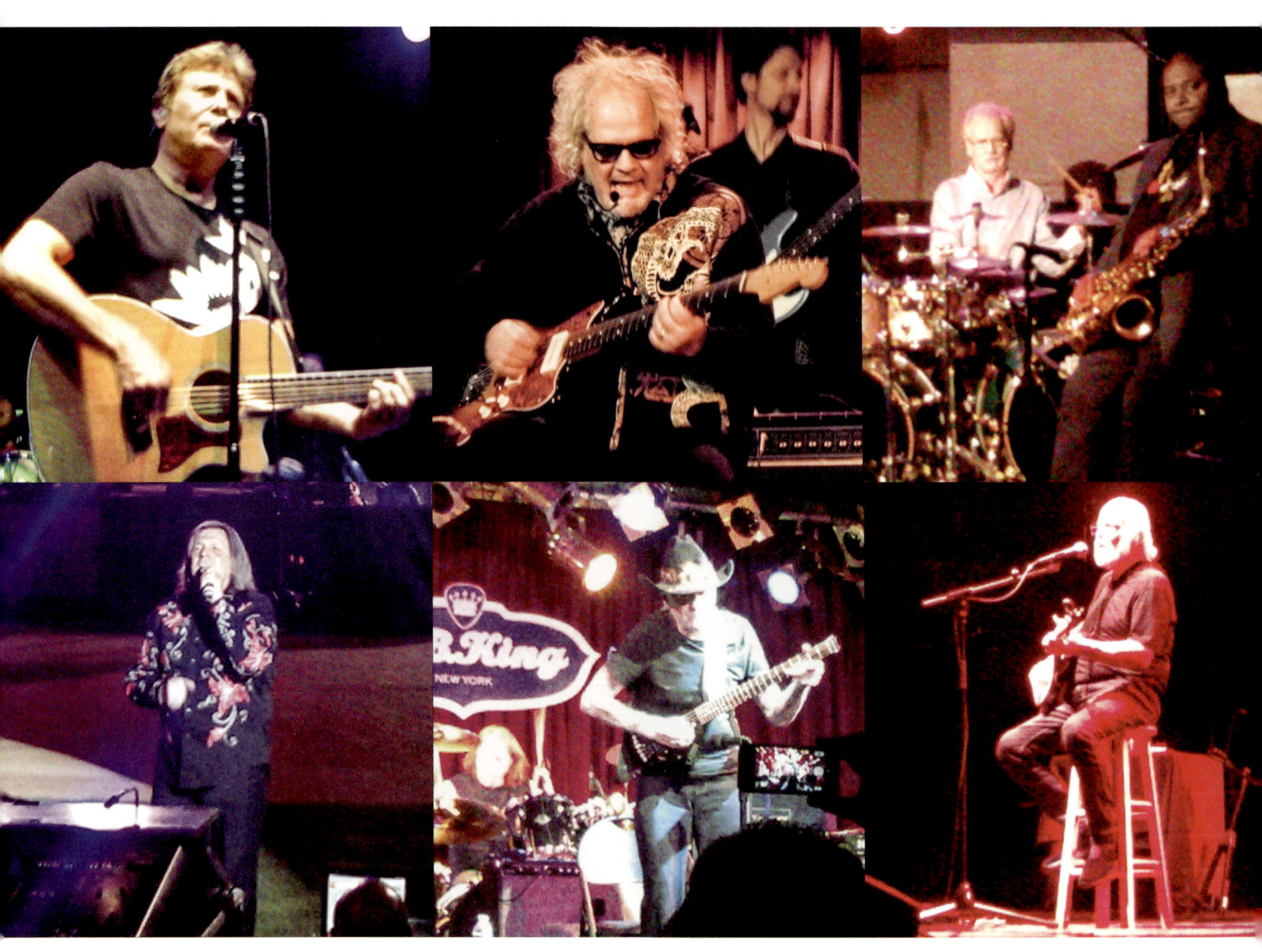

Robert Lamm (Chicago), August 2013

Al Kooper (Blood, Sweat, & Tears; Blues Project), June 2016

Ginger Baker (Cream, Blind Faith), October 2013

Billy J. Kramer and the Dakodas, August 2013

Johnny Winter, January 2013 (RIP d-July 16, 2014)

Robert Hunter (Grateful Dead), October 2013

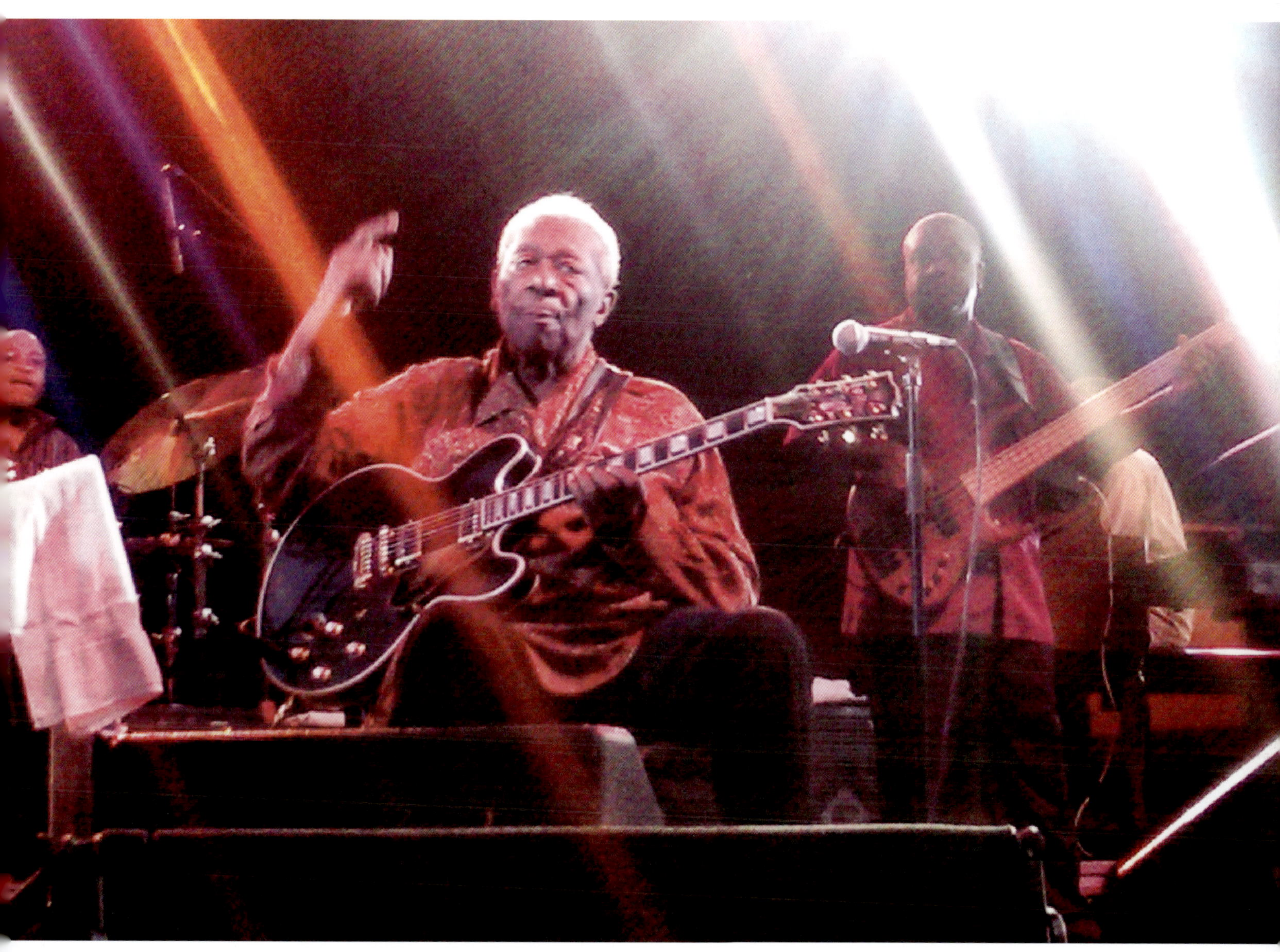

B.B.King, July 2013 (RIP d-May 14, 2015)

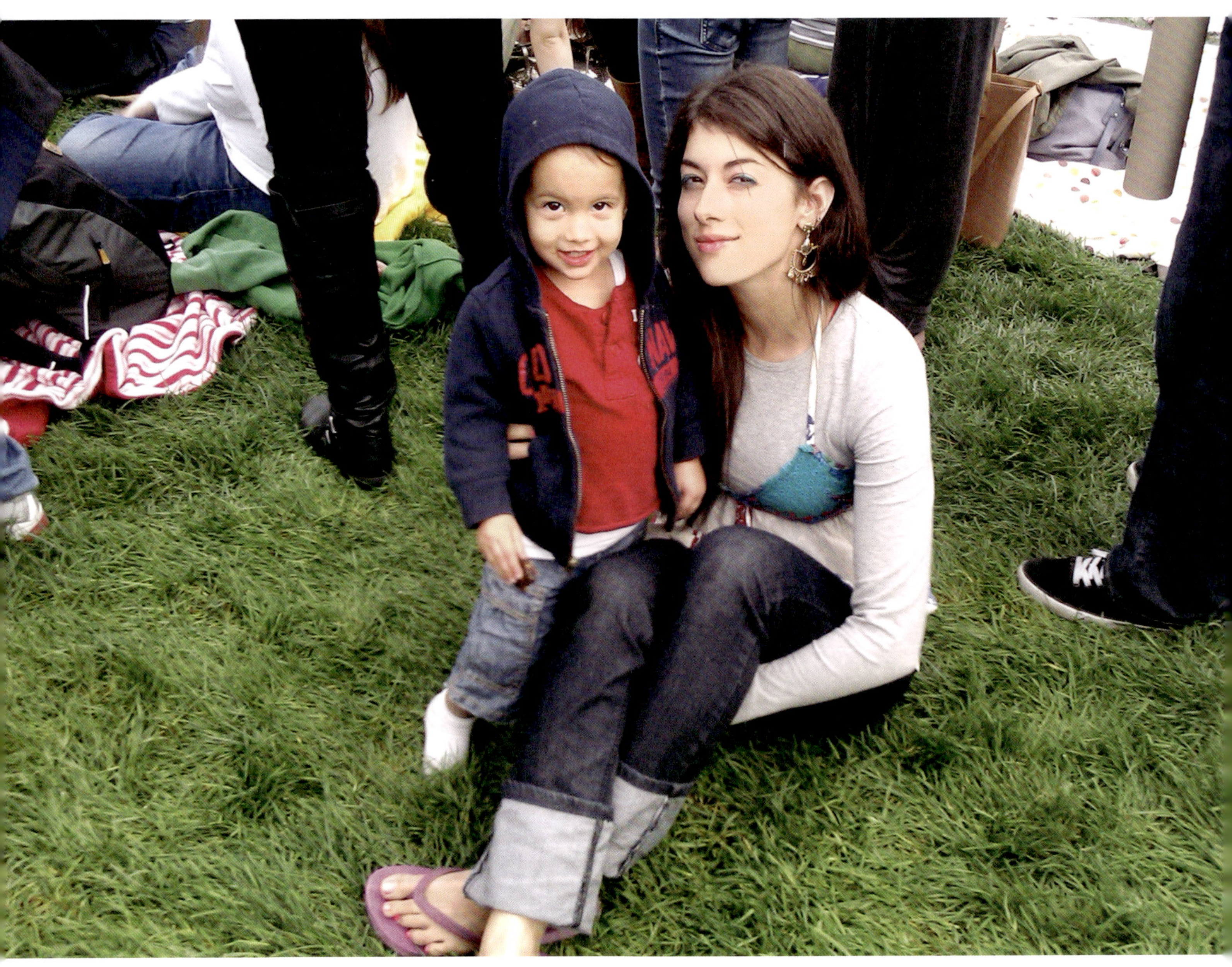

Audience - mother and child at rock fest, September 2013

what music is on the radio than on important things in life, such as spirituality and family. Parents should learn from this and be sure to take more time to give their children a quality education and not let them run wild in the streets. He didn't actually say any of that but that's what he meant.

So the Beatles took time off and stopped touring and concentrated on making music and getting into the studio and expressing their creativity there and the result was Sergeant Pepper's Lonely Hearts Club Band which is the greatest rock album of all time. So thank you Imelda.

When you go to a concert you want to hear your favorite song. Some bands announce before a concert what they are going to play. Steely Dan do a five night show and announce, Monday we'll play Aja; Tuesday-Royal Scam, etc. Then they punch it up by adding a few other hits.

YES said very clearly, 'this show is three full albums, "The Yes Album", "Close To the Edge", and "Going For the One". If you're a YES fan that will just about knock your sock off. Then Roundabout for an encore? Sublime, simply sublime. Renaissance did a similar thing with, "Turn Of the Cards" and "Scheherazade" in their entirety. Heavenly (although my favorite of theirs is "Ashes Are Burning").

But the Grateful Dead, now that's another story. The whole fun of going to see the Grateful Dead is not knowing what they're going to play and then they play your favorite song. But you have a few favorites so it's not too unlikely. I had to see the Dead nine times before I finally got to hear ''St. Stephan'' live.

I saw the Grateful Dead 6 times from 1976 to 1980 (not a lot by Dead Head standards, but respectable). The first concert was in Englishtown New Jersey, just after their new album Terrapin Station came out. There were 125,000 people there. All tripping on acid. The warm-up bands were New Riders of the Purple Sage, and Marshall Tucker Band. It was an all-day event. It was outdoors and it was like Woodstock. Incredible. After the concert people were walking around going to and fro. We didn't know which way to go to get home. I would ask people, 'Excuse me, which is the way out of here'? They all answered the same thing, "I don't know I'm lost". Wandering around in circles for hours. Boy was that fun. What a bunch of crazies.

In 1981 I left the USA and went traveling. I saw very few concerts for about 20 years. I've been to about 90 countries and certainly don't regret it, but I did miss some great concerts (I did get to see Eric Clapton in Jerusalem though). When I returned I certainly never thought I'd see the Grateful Dead again. Poor dear Jerry was no longer with us. But then Rat Dog came to New York and I figured why not? I felt like Rip Van Winkle. There I was back in the whole Grateful Dead scene like I'd never left. Rapture. Since then I also saw Phil and Friends (Phil Lesh the Grateful Dead's bass player and his band), and Robert Hunter (who writes the lyrics and plays guitar and sings solo- a must see for anyone who loves the Grateful Dead). There is also Further (Bob Weir and Phil Lesh together) and Mickey Hart (their multitalented drummer) to see, so the Grateful Dead experience is still widely available, 50 years after their first album was released.

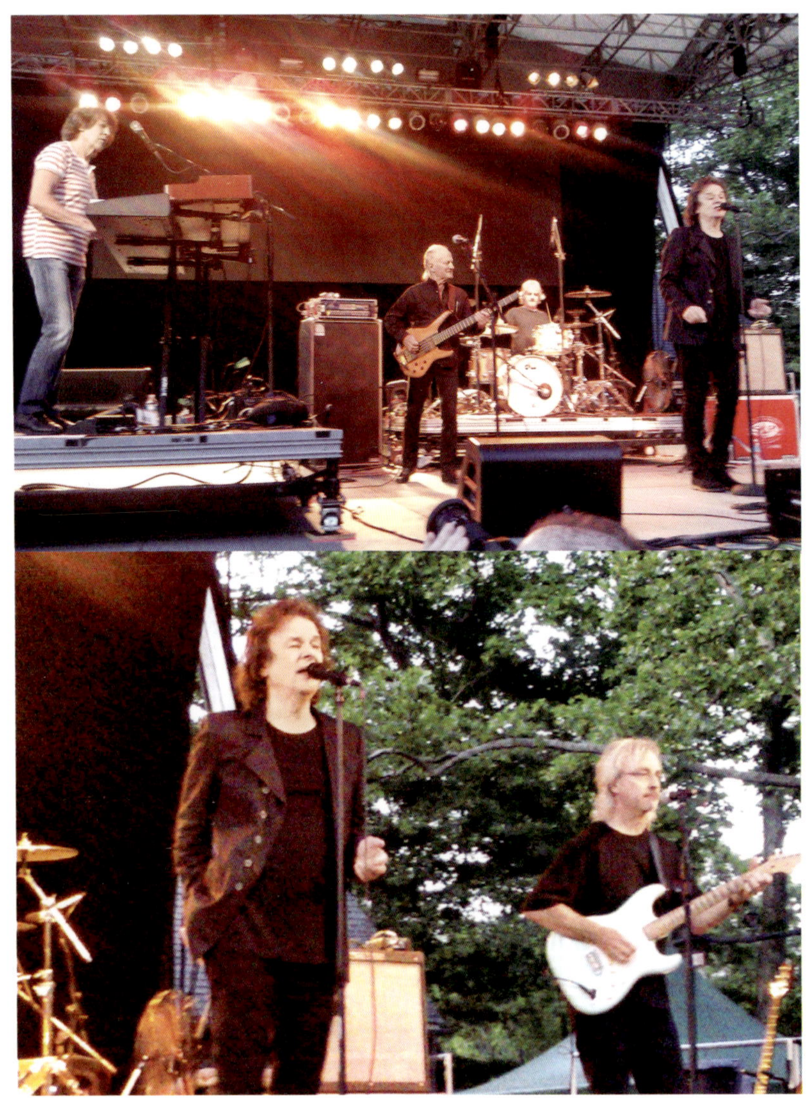

The Zombies, June 2013

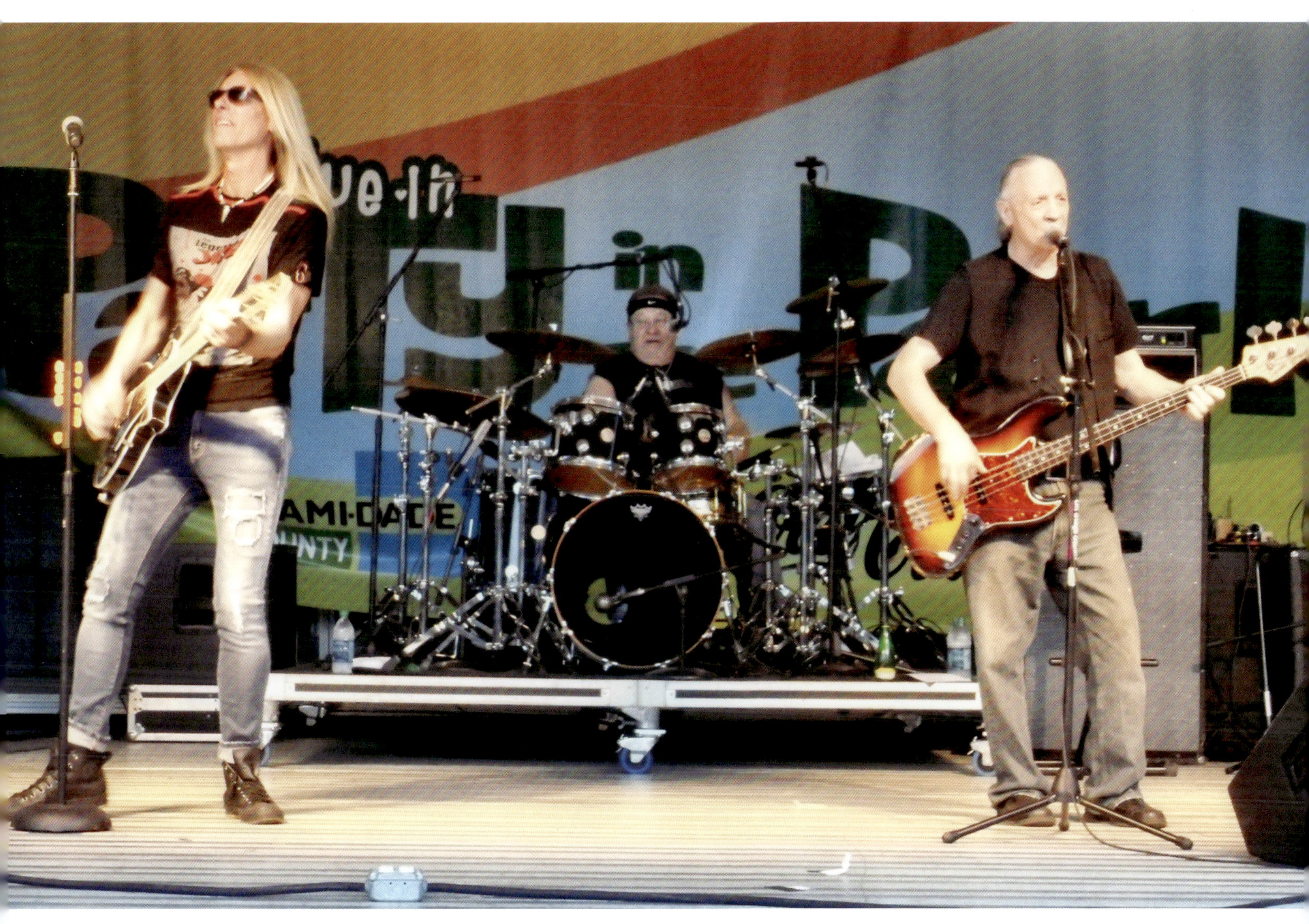

The Guess Who, May 2015

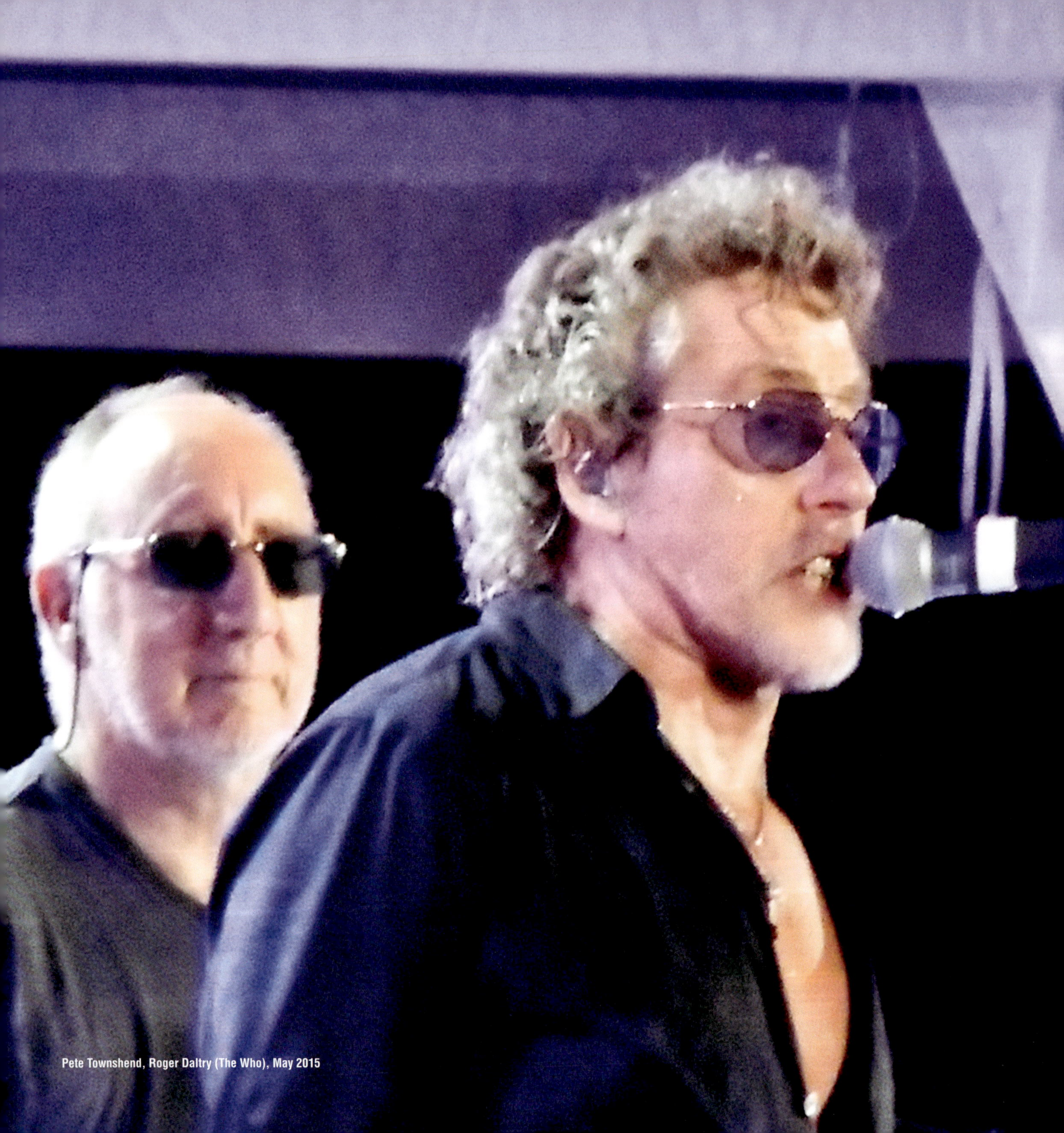

Pete Townshend, Roger Daltry (The Who), May 2015

But the most noticeable thing about these post-Jerry Dead Shows is that the audience is young! A whole new generation of Dead-Heads is upon us. At Steely Dan and Yes everyone is in their fifties. It's the same audience you had when they were first starting out. The guys you were sitting next to in 1978 are sitting next to you now!

But the Dead-Heads are multigenerational. Sure there are some, what do they call us? 'elders' still around, and it's good to be respected as they do, knowing that we built the foundation for this very show that you're at, but mostly it's new hippies! So it's really like it was when I first saw them. A bunch of crazy kids dancing. I saw Robert Plant recently. The audience was a bunch of crazy kids, yes, but we were all in our 50s. What a thrill to see Robert Plant sing ''Whole Lotta Love'' and ''When the Levy Breaks''. After the show this 50 -or-so-year-old lady is trying to wake up her 14-year-old son and drag him out of there. She's shuddering with delight and the kid's sleeping through the show.

She finally gets him up and starts making for the door. You can see he's bored to tears. She obviously so wanted to share her greatest joy with her undisciplined issue and it wasn't quite working out. I said to the kid, "say, do you realize you just saw history? I mean this is like seeing George Washington. This is the man that invented Heavy Metal. He invented 'cool'". He seemed actually somewhat impressed with that (being as it wasn't coming from his mother) and smiled. The mother looked at me and almost started to weep.

And speaking of talking to folks at concerts and the Grateful Dead, I always enjoy talking to other audience members and getting their views and the overall vibe. So at Phil Lesh and Friends I got quite a surprise by the 'overall vibe' by getting the exact same story from several disparate fans. "So how'd you like the show?" "Oh, it was great. Y'know, Ratdog (ex Dead member Bob Weir's band) is great and everything, and the last Further (Bob Weir and Phil Lesh together with other ex Dead members and new members) show was outrageous and all, but… Bobby is just a bit too domineering. He just can't help taking over. Phil is so mellow. I think I like the Phil shows better." They seem almost like they feel guilty for liking the Phil Lesh shows better than the Bob Weir shows, even when Phil Lesh is together with Bob Weir. And I had this exact same spontaneous conversation with several completely different fans. It's the vibe.

Well no wonder they feel guilty for even thinking a disparaging thought for Bob Weir. And it's not even disparaging or in any way acrimonious. It's only when comparing him to someone else. Because Bob Weir, together with Jerry Garcia and the rest of the Grateful Dead, pretty much invented the hippies. He made you what you are and love most. San Francisco in the early 60s. The Grateful Dead, the Jefferson Airplane. The music was the engine that forged the protest movement of the 60s and defined pop culture for young people. There was a clear 'generation gap' at that time, as it was called. 'Don't trust anyone over 30', was the motto of the 60s. It was all about counter-culture and anti-establishment. And the music and concerts were the manifestation of the ideas. Going to a rock concert was not a form of entertainment. It was a statement. It meant you were protesting the war in Vietnam in general and fed up with the older generation and their values in particular.

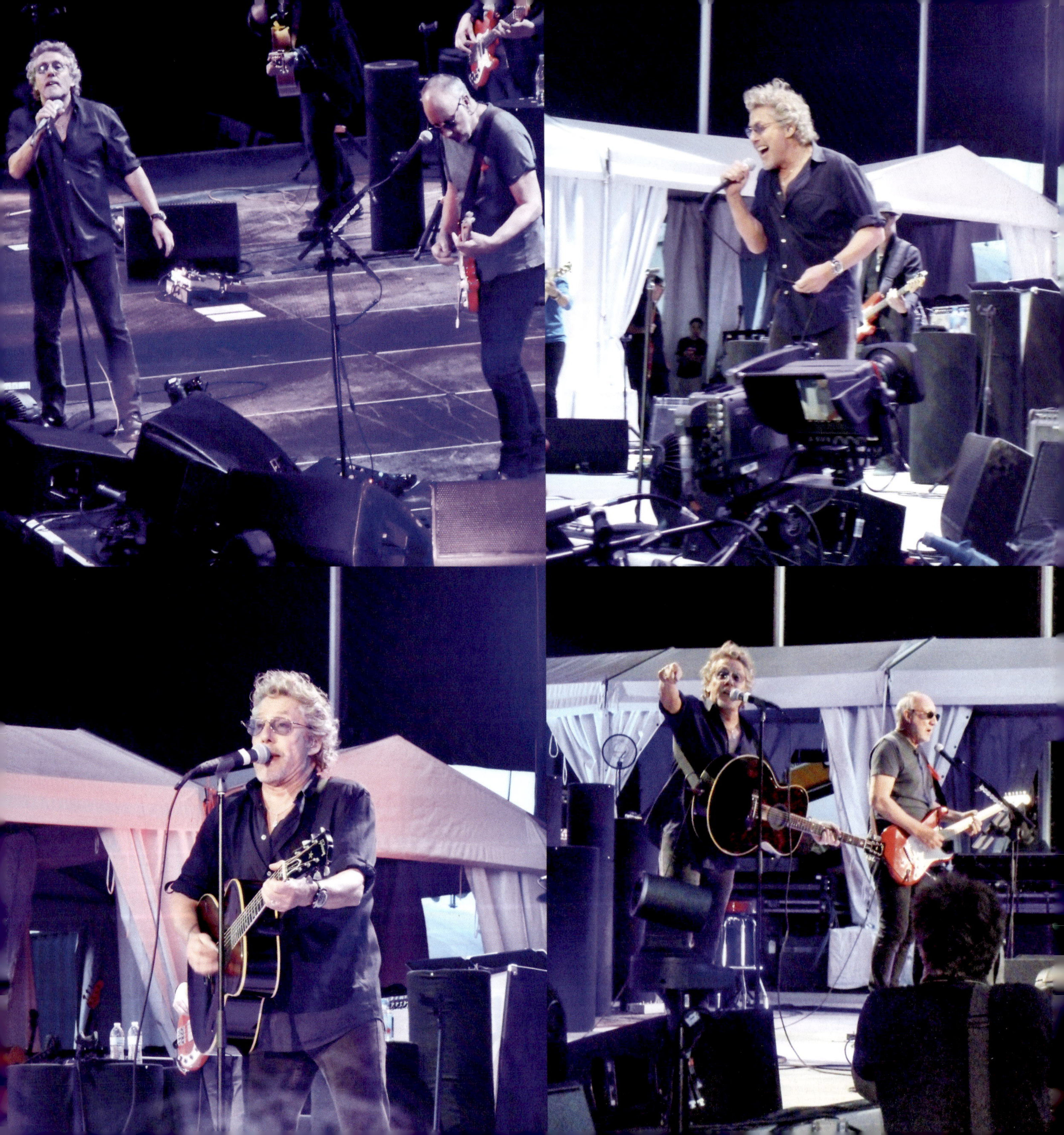

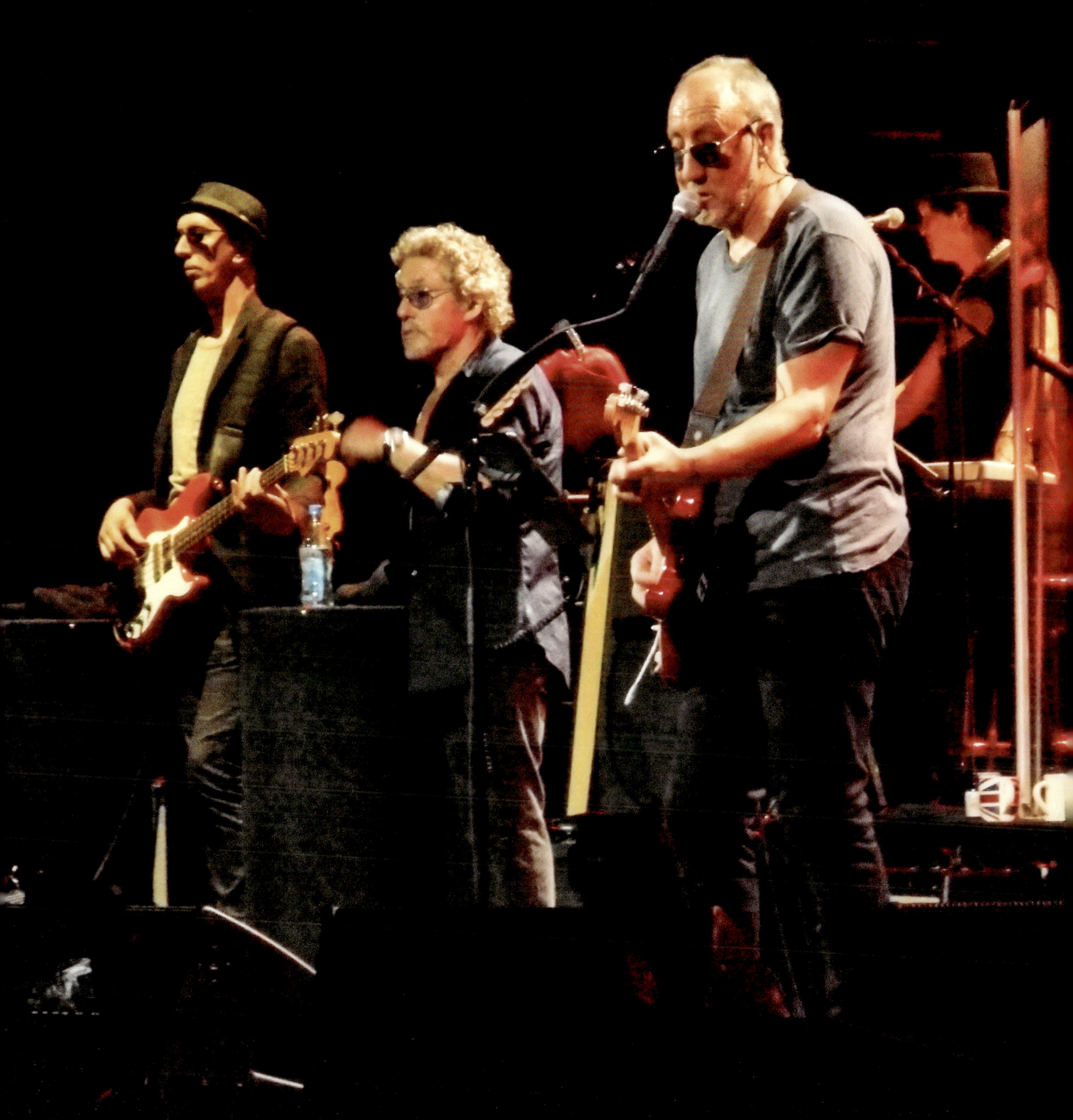

Love-in's, Be-in's, Human Be-in's, protests, sit-in's, draft-card burnings, etc etc. It was the Roaring 20s all over again. You don't remember the 20s but I do. The 20s was also about protesting and surviving the war (the World War aka WWI) and about challenging long established custom, and having more leisure time, and prosperity, and experimenting with new drugs and women wearing drastically less clothes, and sexual promiscuity, and out with the old, in with the new. And the 20s were not the first time this had happened either. It has been the familiar pendulum of the evolution of society since the advent of civilization. And music is the time capsule that is the thermometer of pop-culture.

Shakespeare said, "All the world's a stage" (As You Like It -act II scene VII). Being at a rock concert is not only being an audience, it's being an activist. So when you're at a concert you're on stage, in the audience, watching, doing, and sometimes doing drugs. That's a lot of activity for just sitting there. But before you know it you're not sitting there, you're up on your feet and dancing. It's impossible to sit down at some concerts. You just can't. The guy in front of you is standing so you have to stand too if you want to see. But more, it's not enough to just watch, you have to do, to dance, to cheer, to be part of it actively, proactively, and to show support and love for your favorite singers, musicians, and song writers. Because they cause so much joy in your life that you want to return it. What if everybody just sat there? Paul might get sad. That would be unacceptable.

So in the 200th row in Madison Square Garden a block from Mars you stand up and clap and dance so Paul will see you. But he doesn't see you, does he? But he does, he feels the energy and it's a thrill and the performer gets a little bit of all the collective joy that the entire house feels because he caused it. So he'll do it again and again. So back there a mile from the stage you're making a difference, a big difference, to the house, to the world. But why be a mile away? Move up to the front! Where you can get a decent picture. Then once you get a decent shot put the silly camera away. And enjoy the show. Enjoy the moment. Enjoy the Now. Because this moment will only occur once. So make the most of it. That's the power and beauty of music, and of a great show. You can forget the past and future and be in this moment. This moment of joy and wonder.

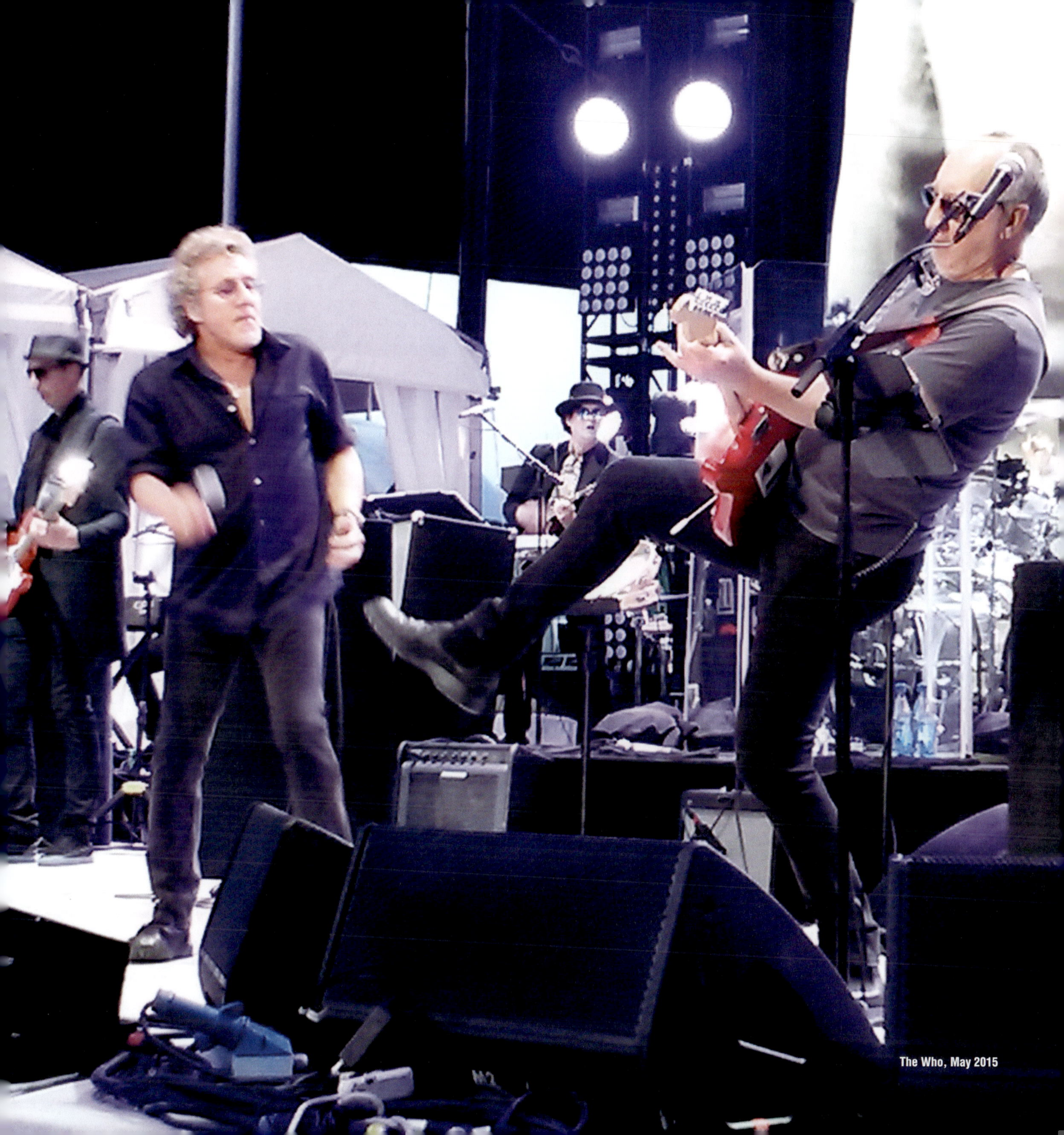

The Who, May 2015

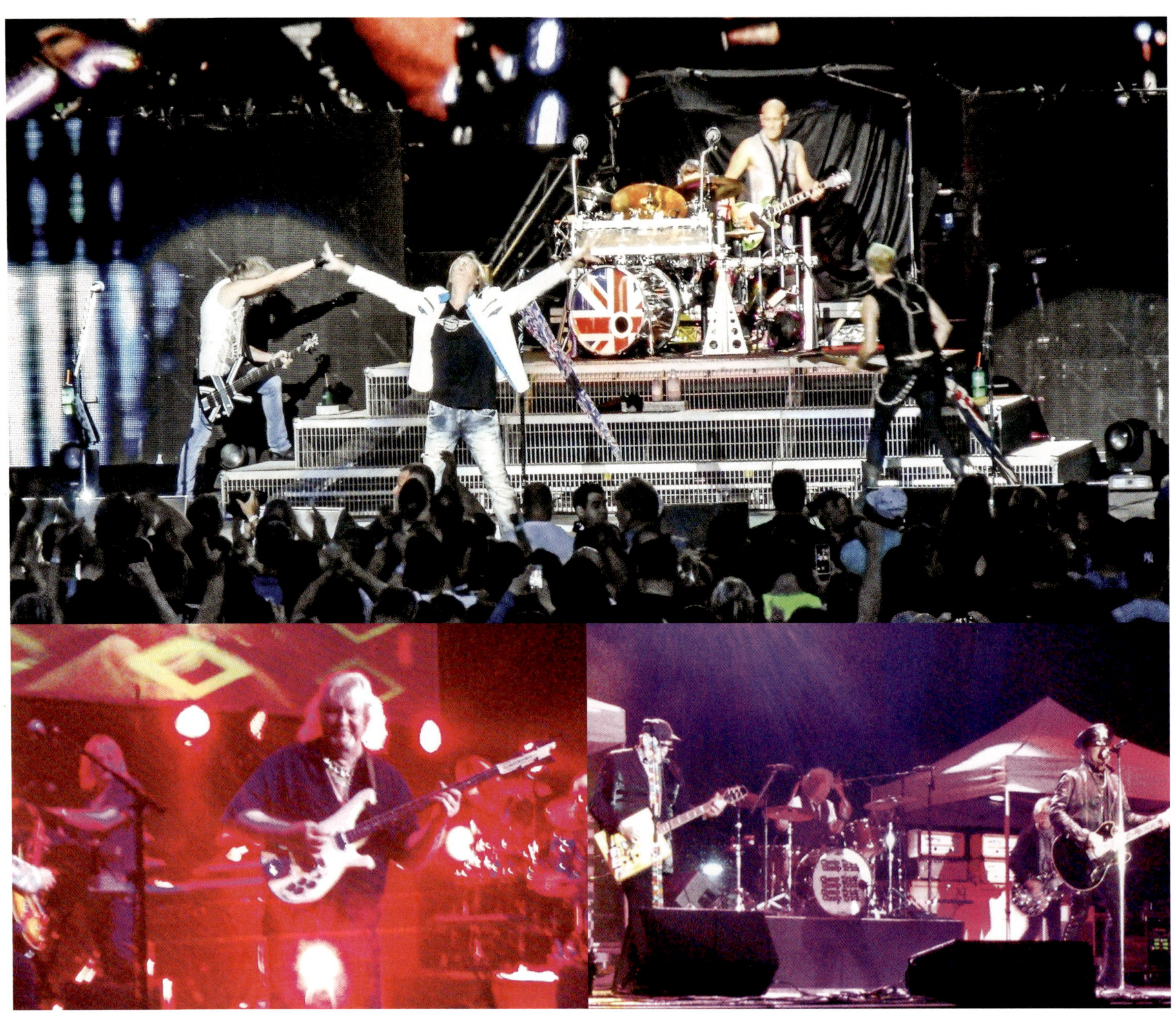

Def Leppard, August 2014

Chris Squire (Yes), July 2013 (RIP d-June 27, 2015)                    Cheap Trick, July 2013

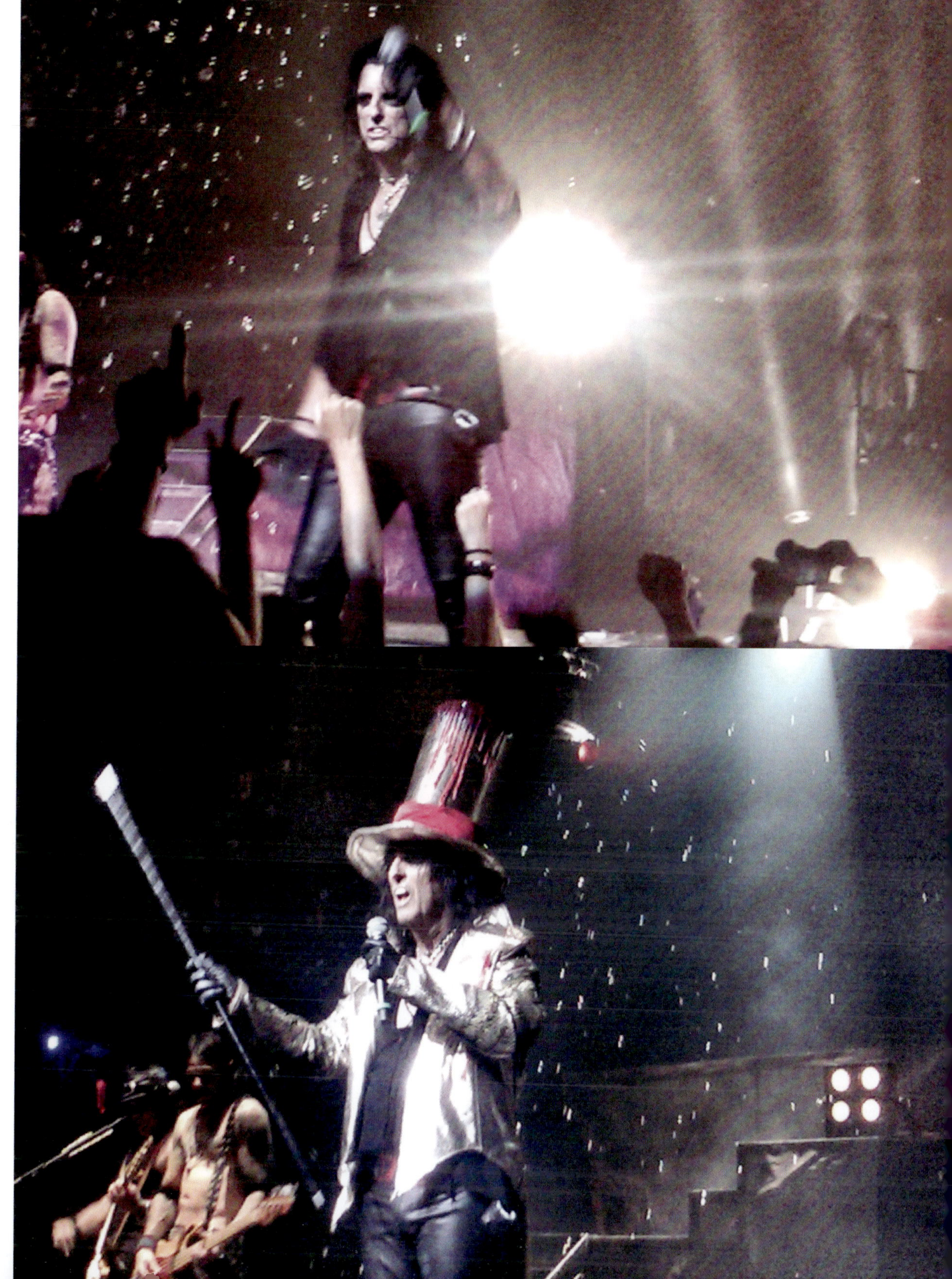

Alice Cooper, July 2013

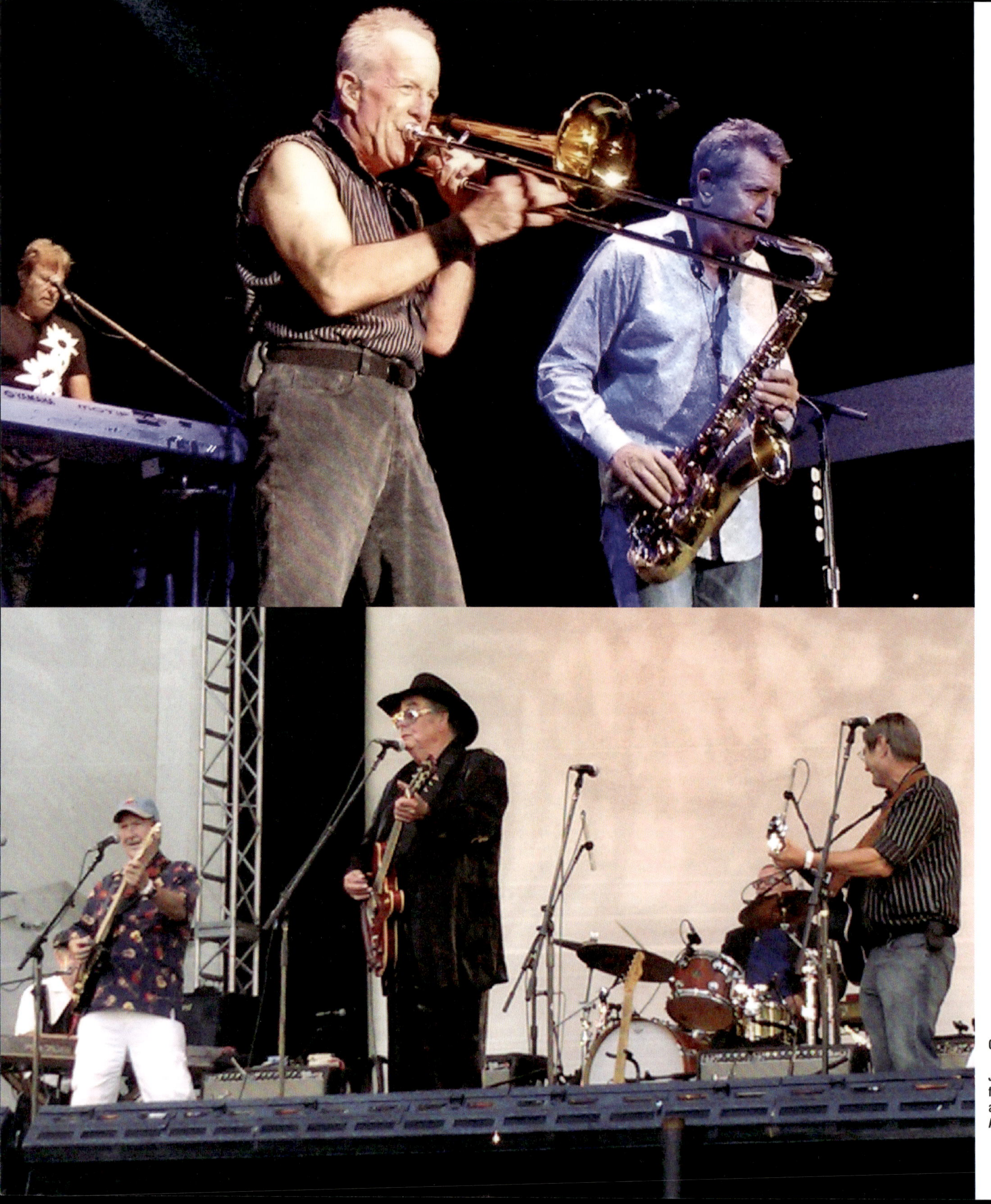

Chicago, August 2013

James Burton (Guitarist for Elvis Presley's Band and Sleepy LaBeef, August 2013

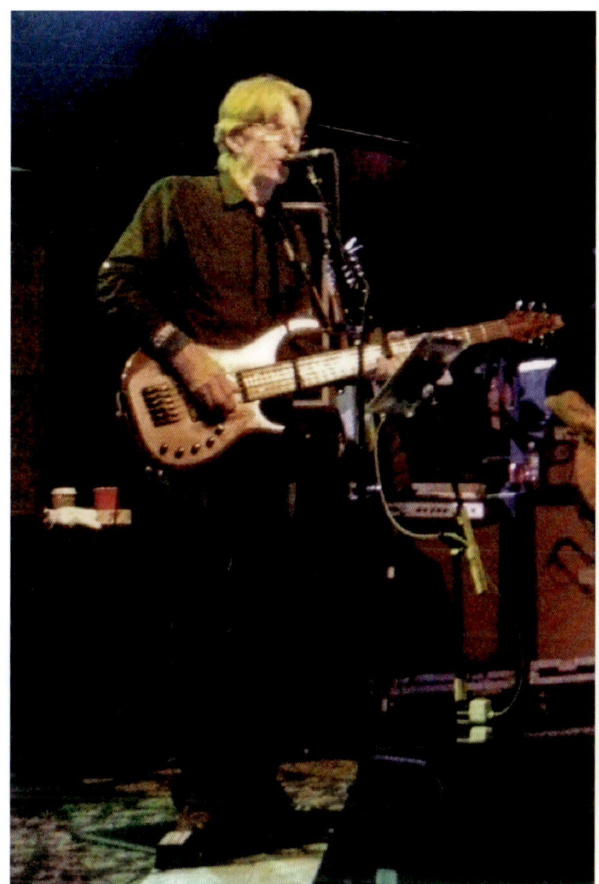

Phil Lesh (Grateful Dead), November 2013

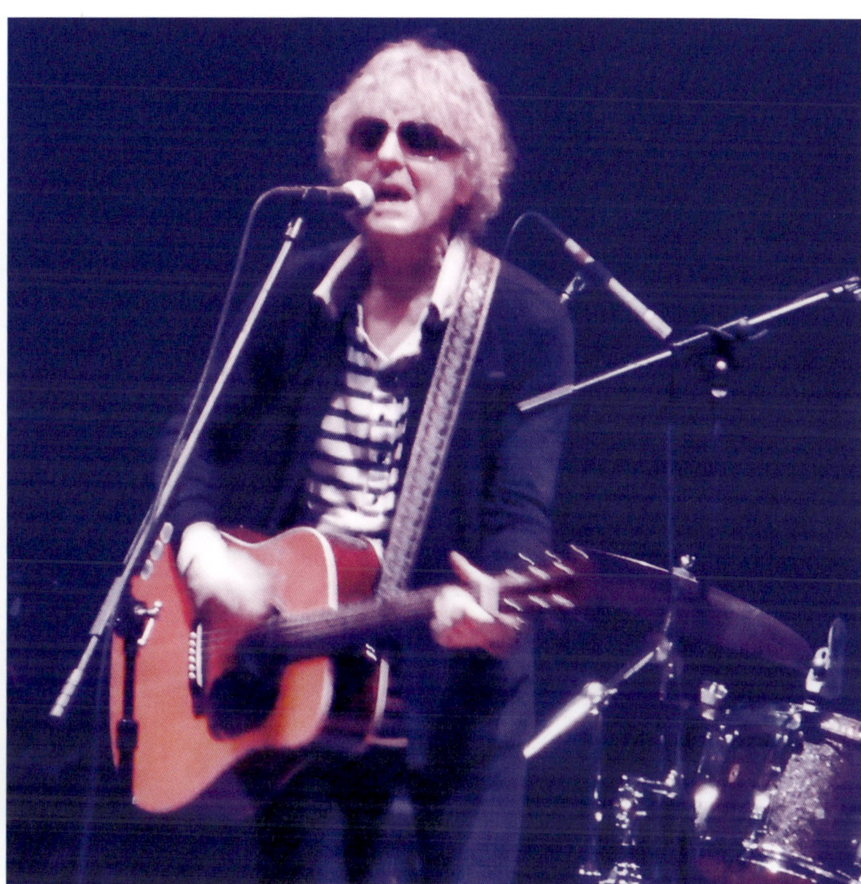

Ian Hunter (Mott the Hoople), August 2015

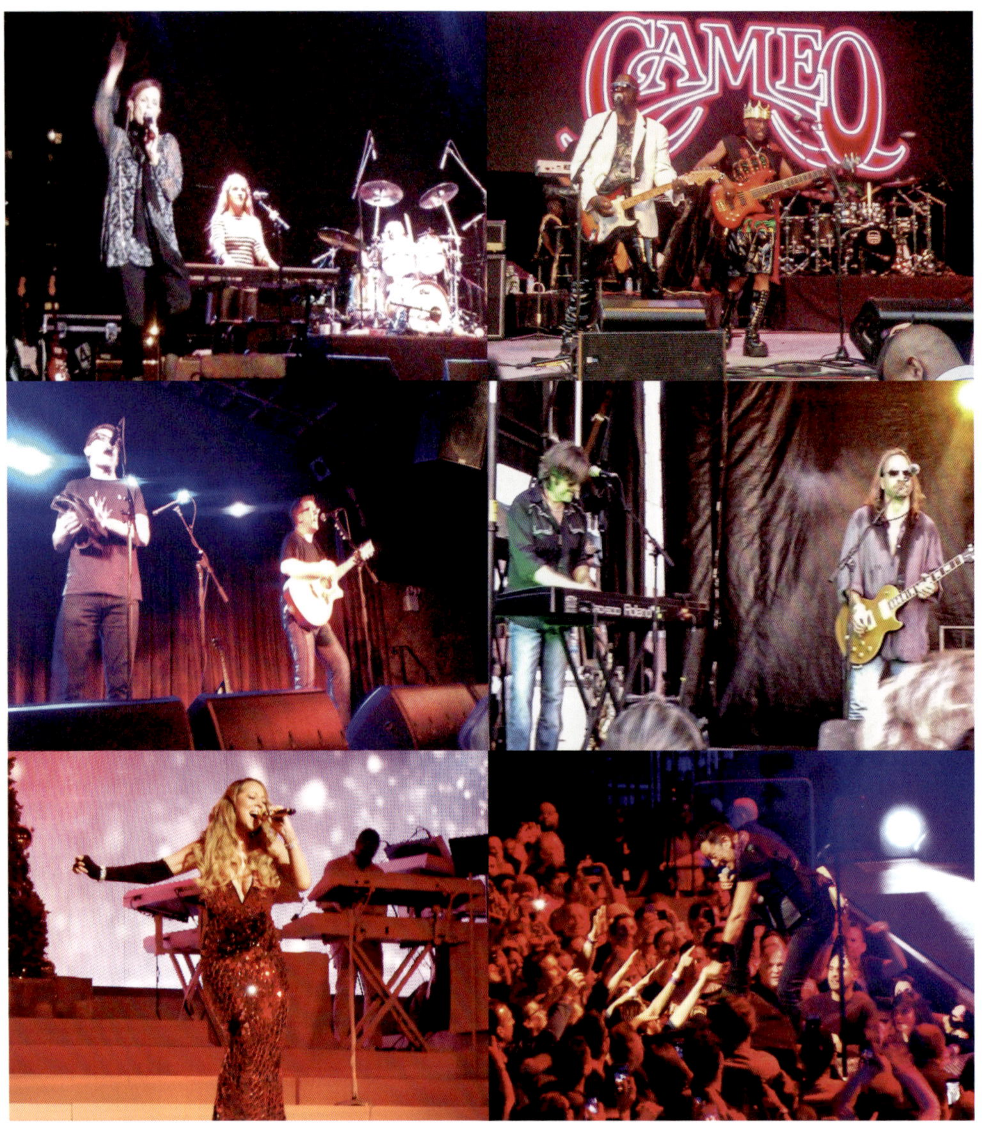

Belinda Carlyle, The Go Go's, August 2013

Cameo, July 2013

The Proclaimers, April 2013

Marshall Tucker Band, October 2012

Mariah Carey, December 2015

Bruce Springsteen, April 2016

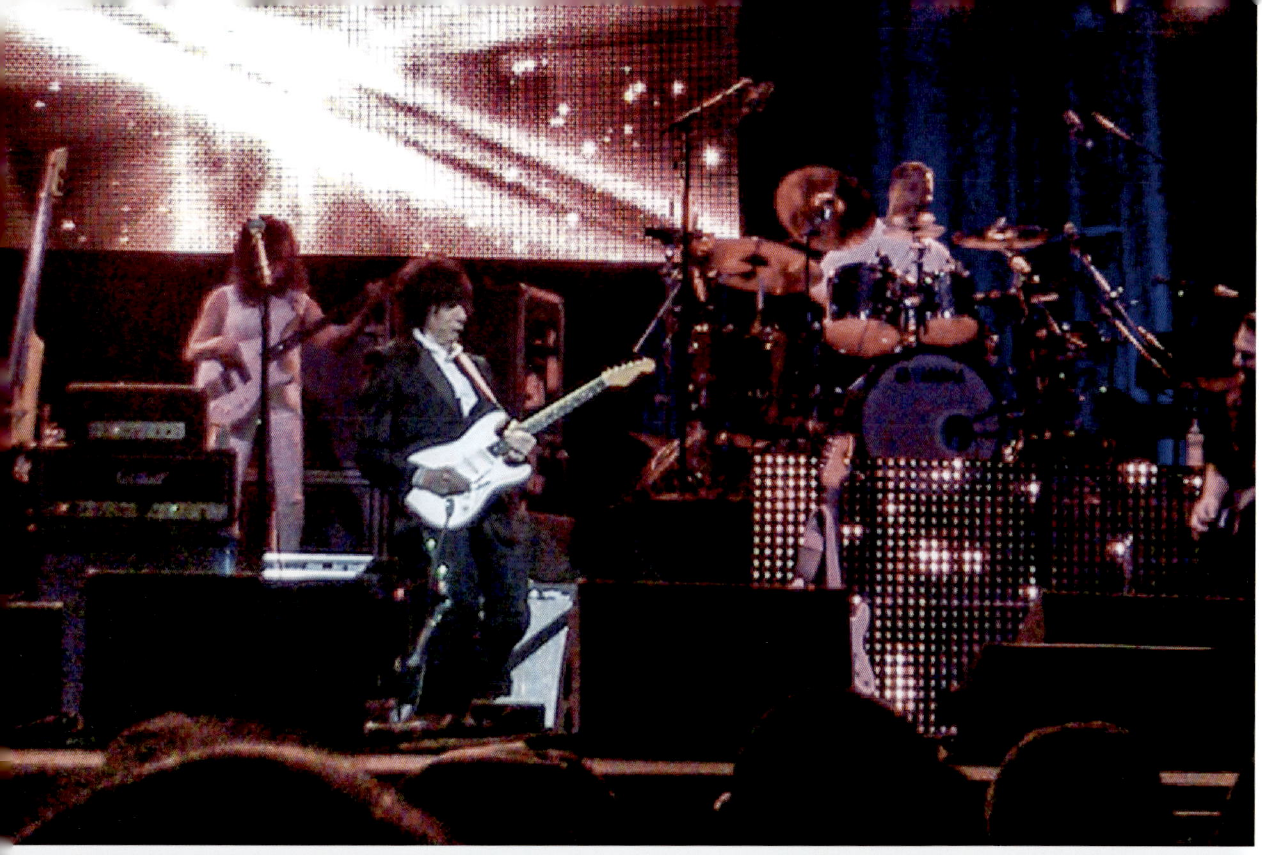

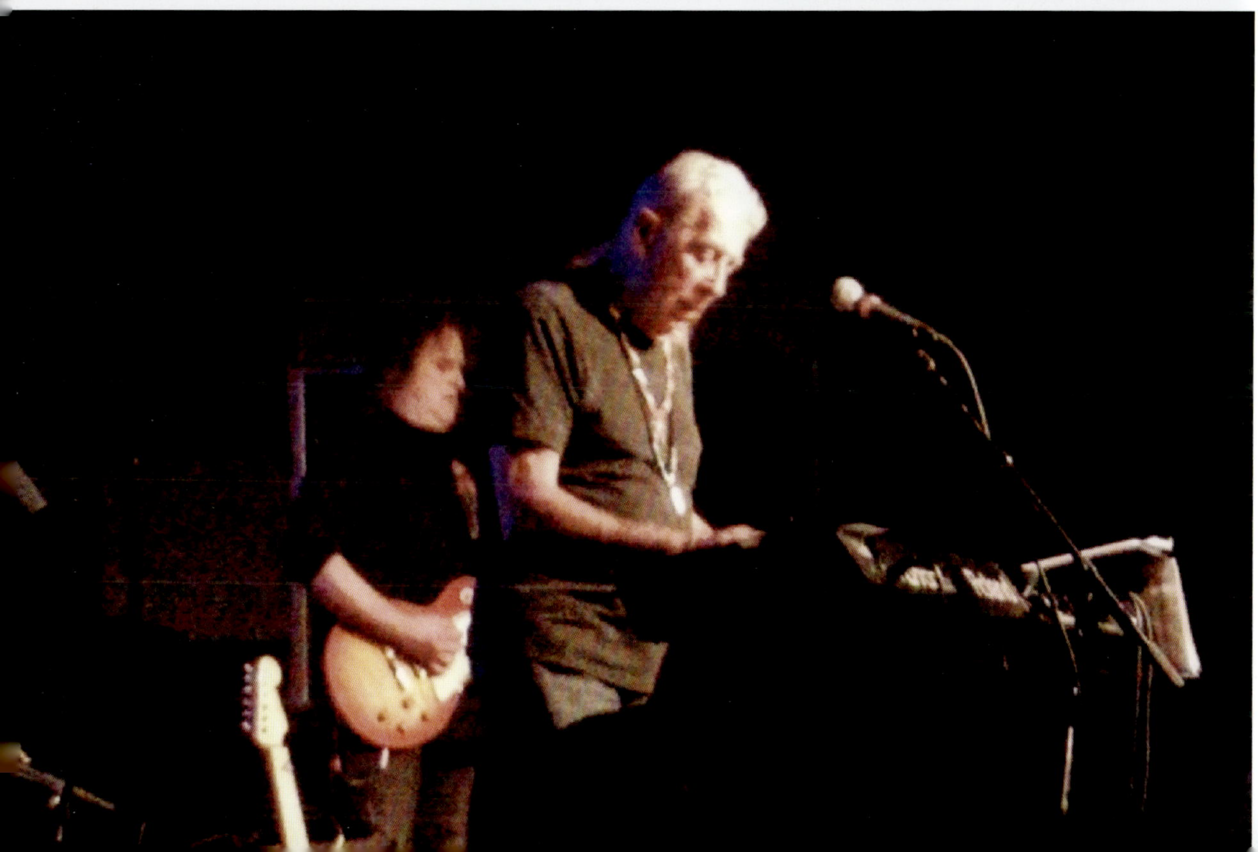

Jeff Beck, October 2013

John Mayall (Blues Breakers),
October 2013

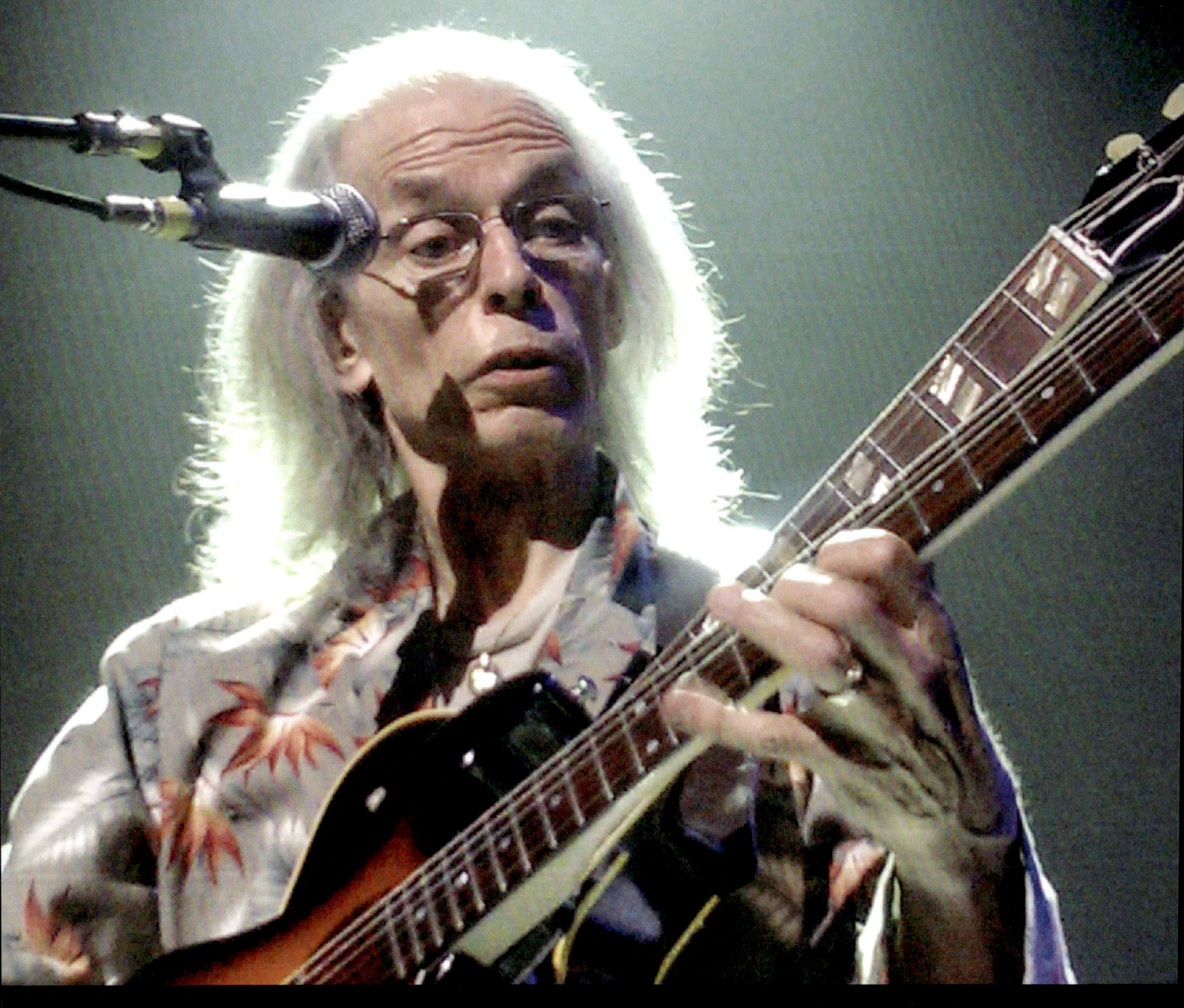

Steve Howe (Yes, Asia), July 2013

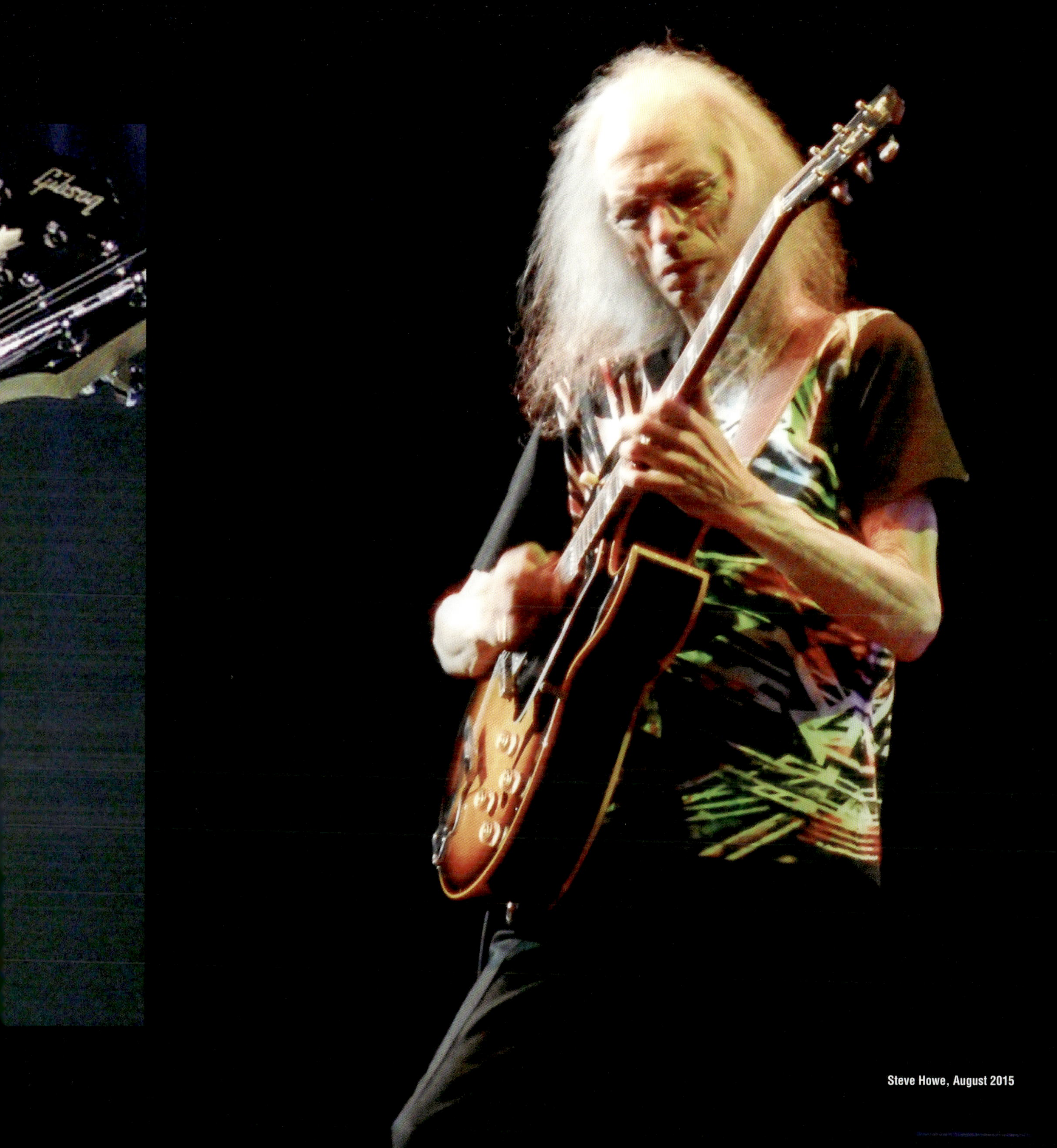

Steve Howe, August 2015

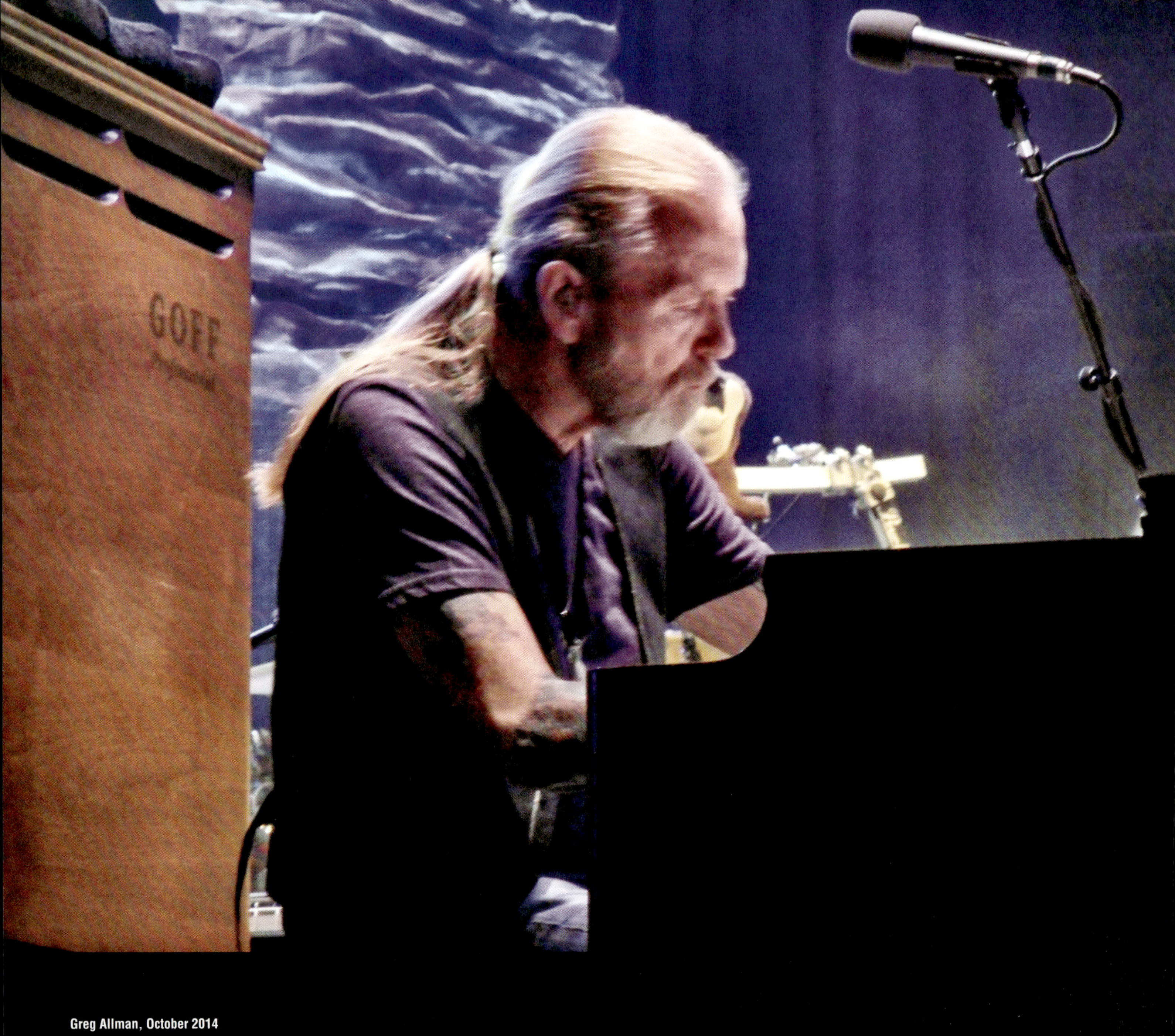

Greg Allman, October 2014

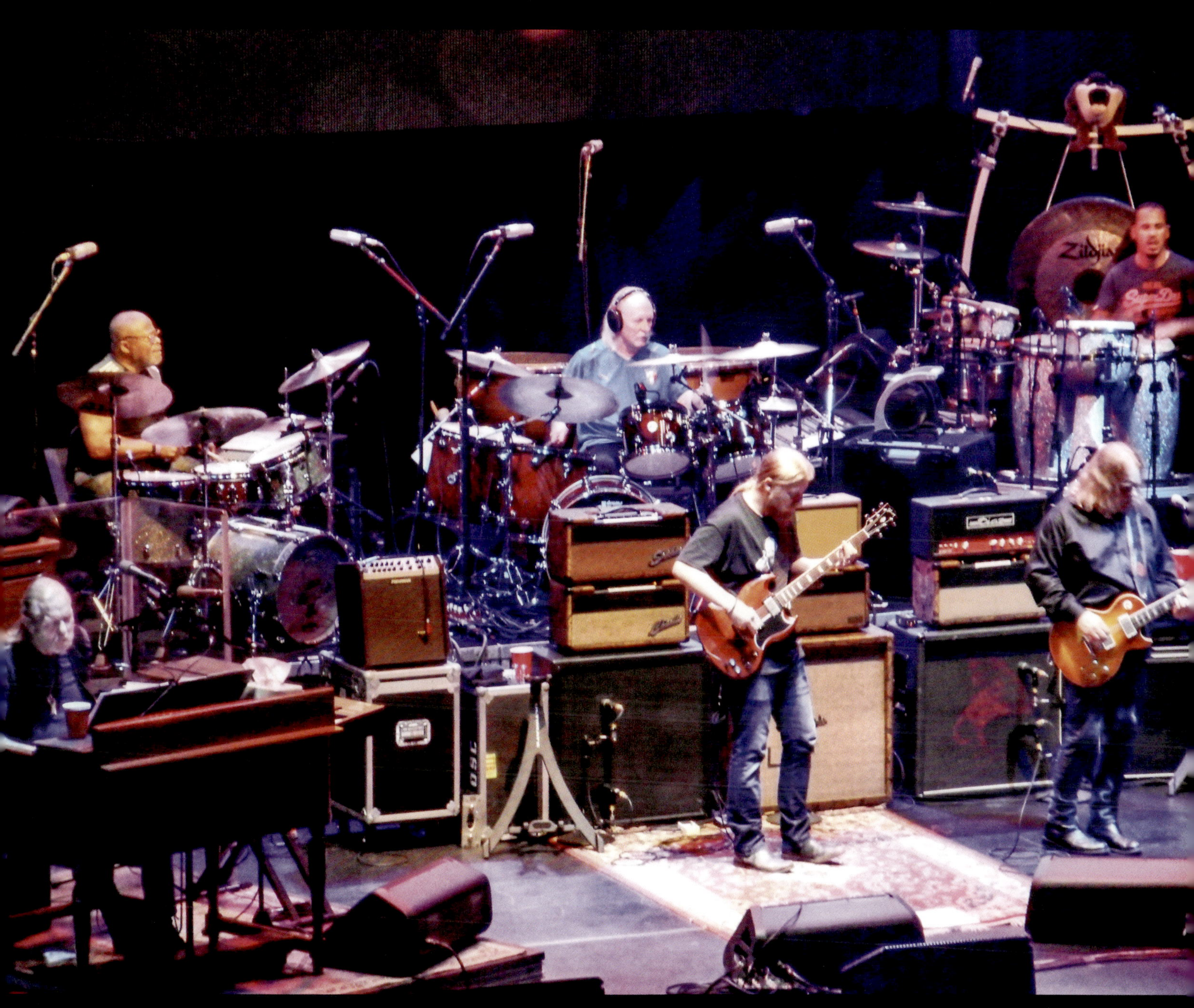

Allman Brothers, October 2014

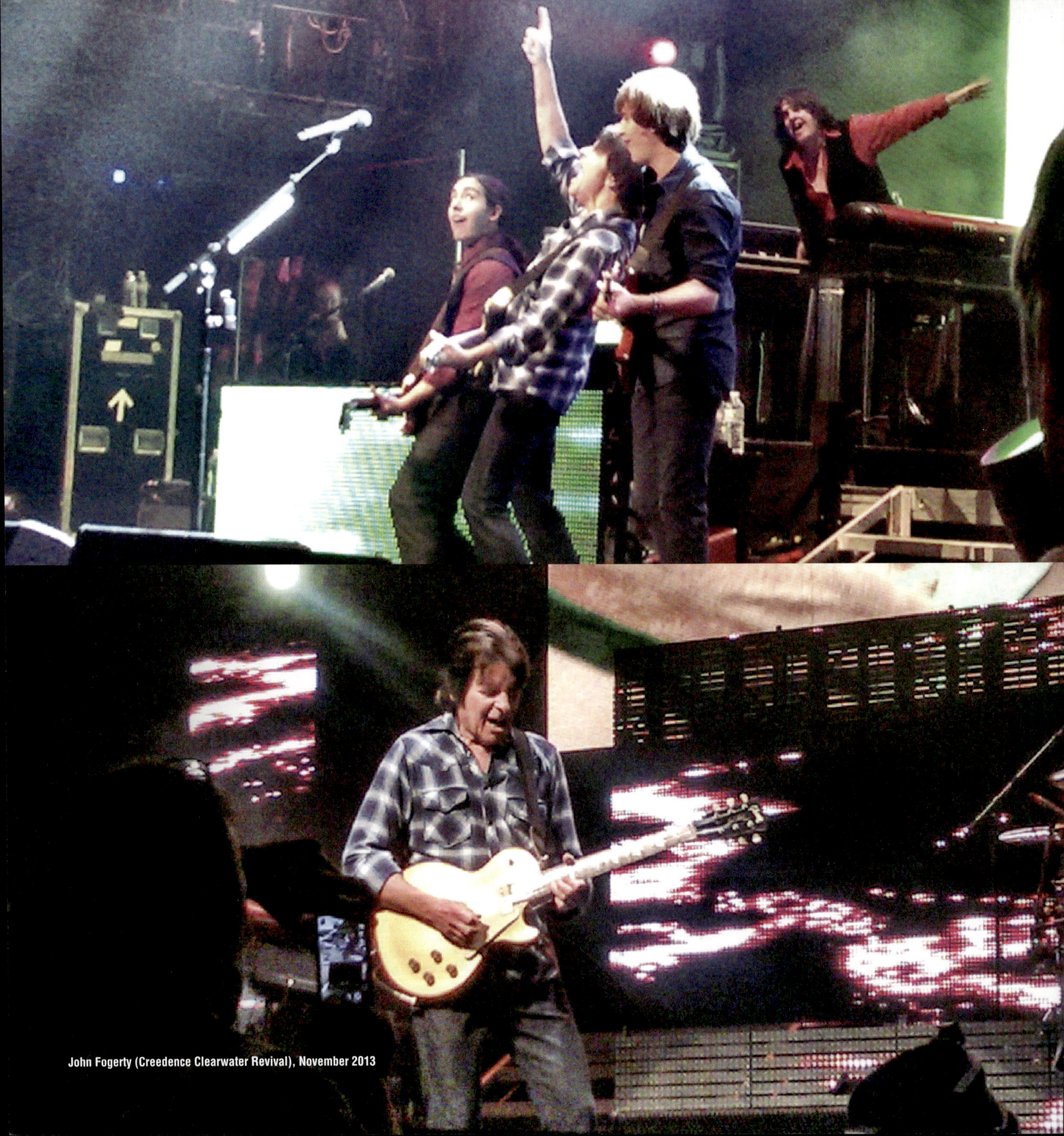
John Fogerty (Creedence Clearwater Revival), November 2013

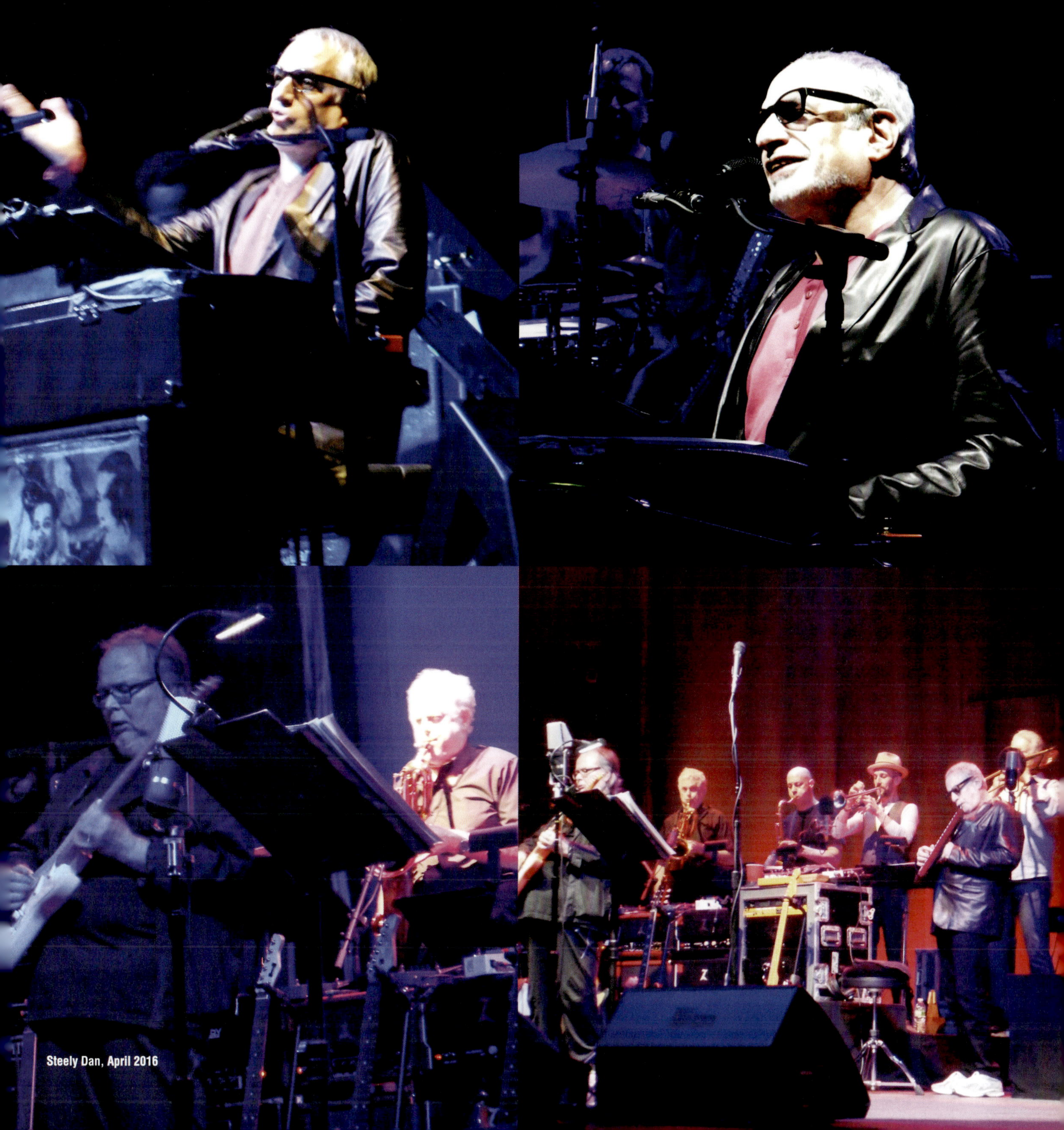

Steely Dan, April 2016

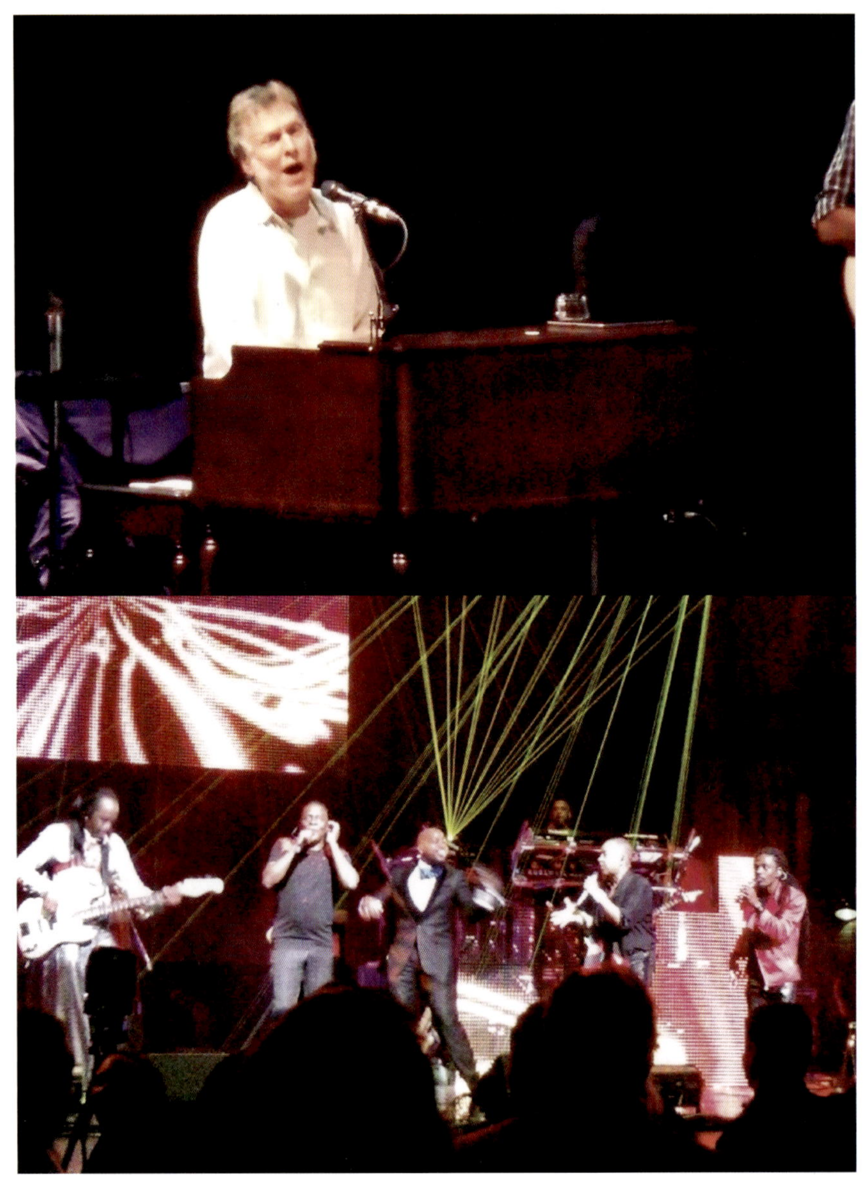

Steve Winwood (Spencer Davis Group, Blind Faith, Traffic), September 2014

Earth, Wind and Fire, September 2013

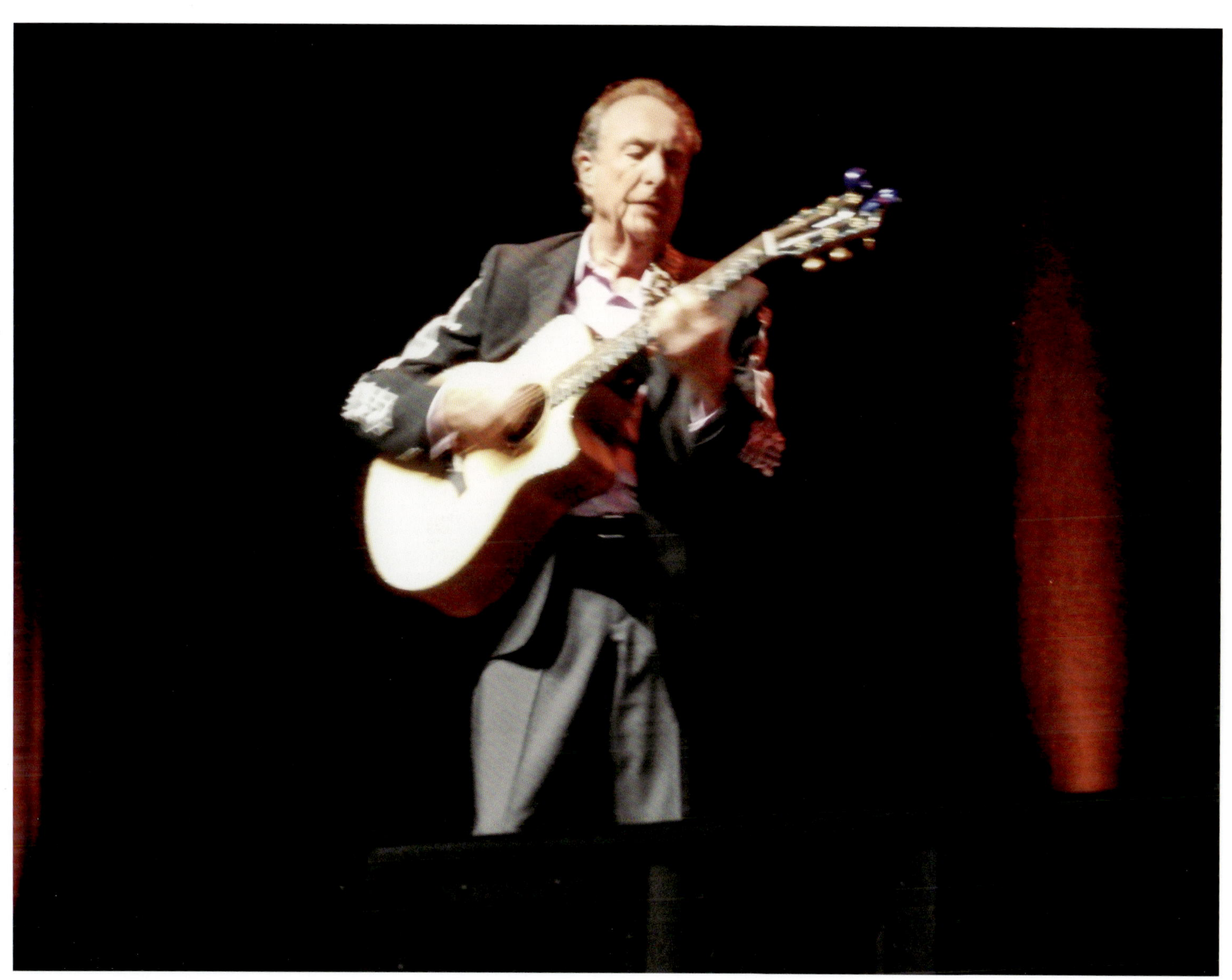

Eric Idle (The Rutles, Monty Python, Spamalot), October 2015

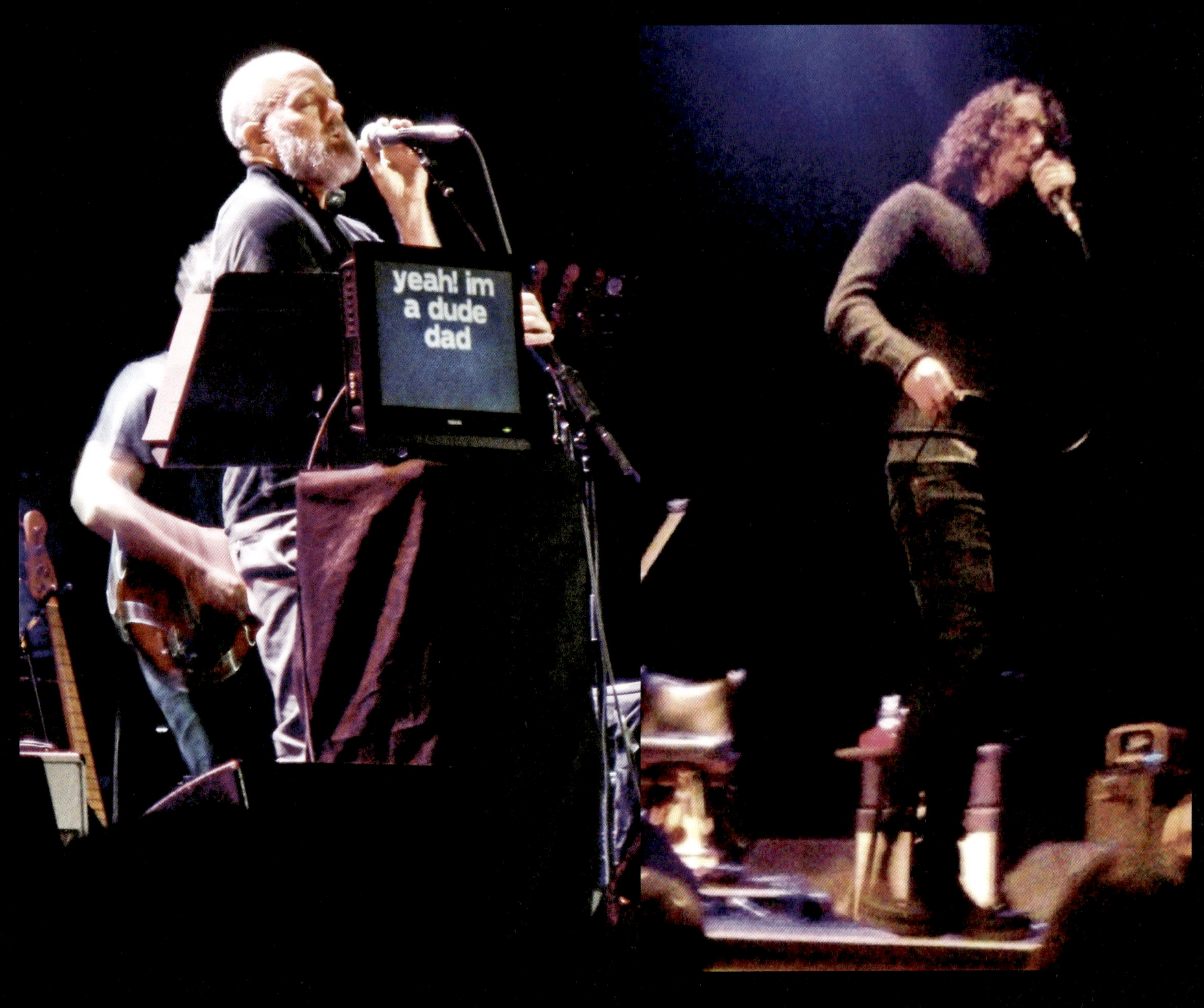


Michael Stipe (R.E.M.), November 2015

Chris Cornell (Soundgarden), November 2013

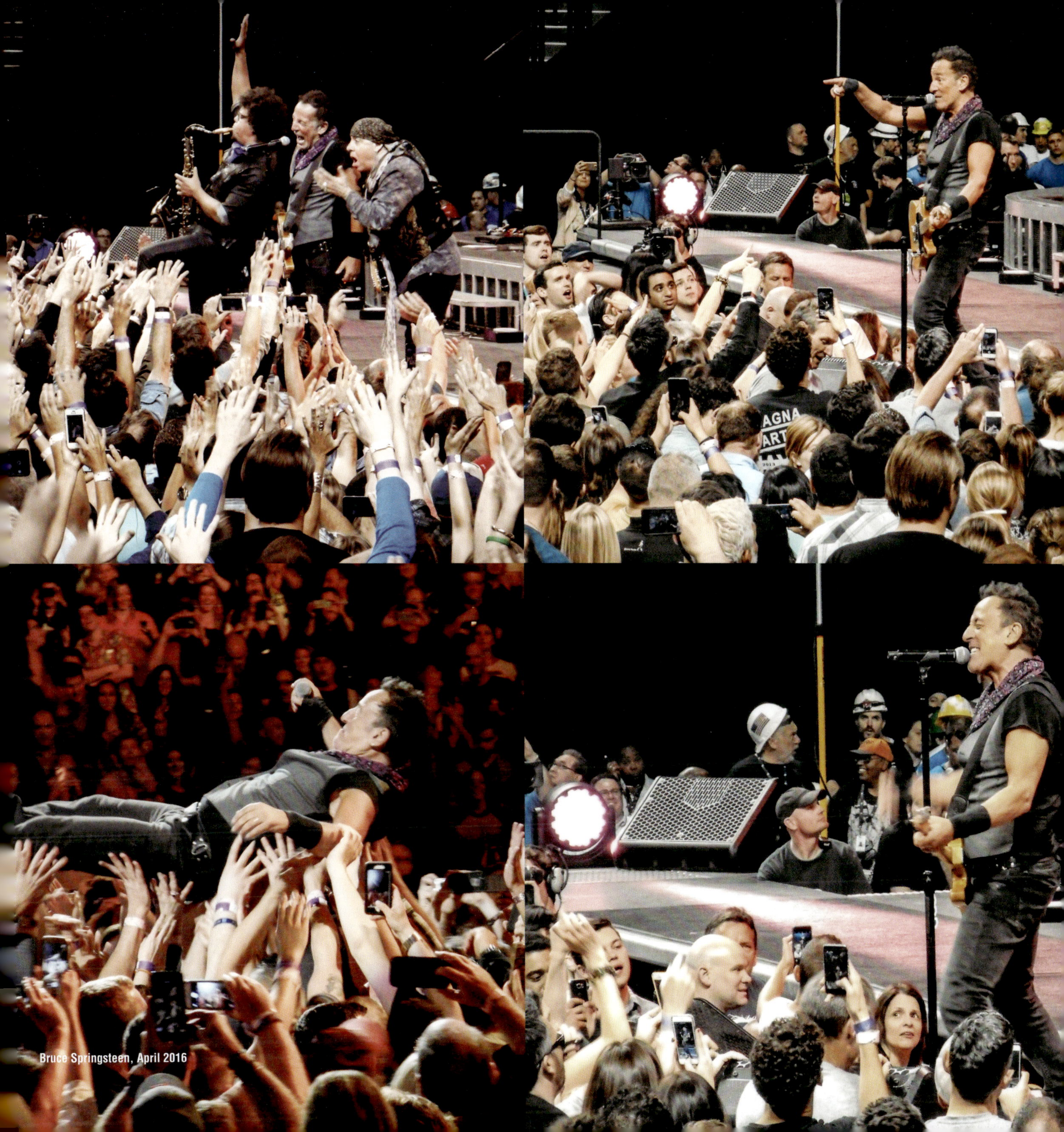

Bruce Springsteen, April 2016

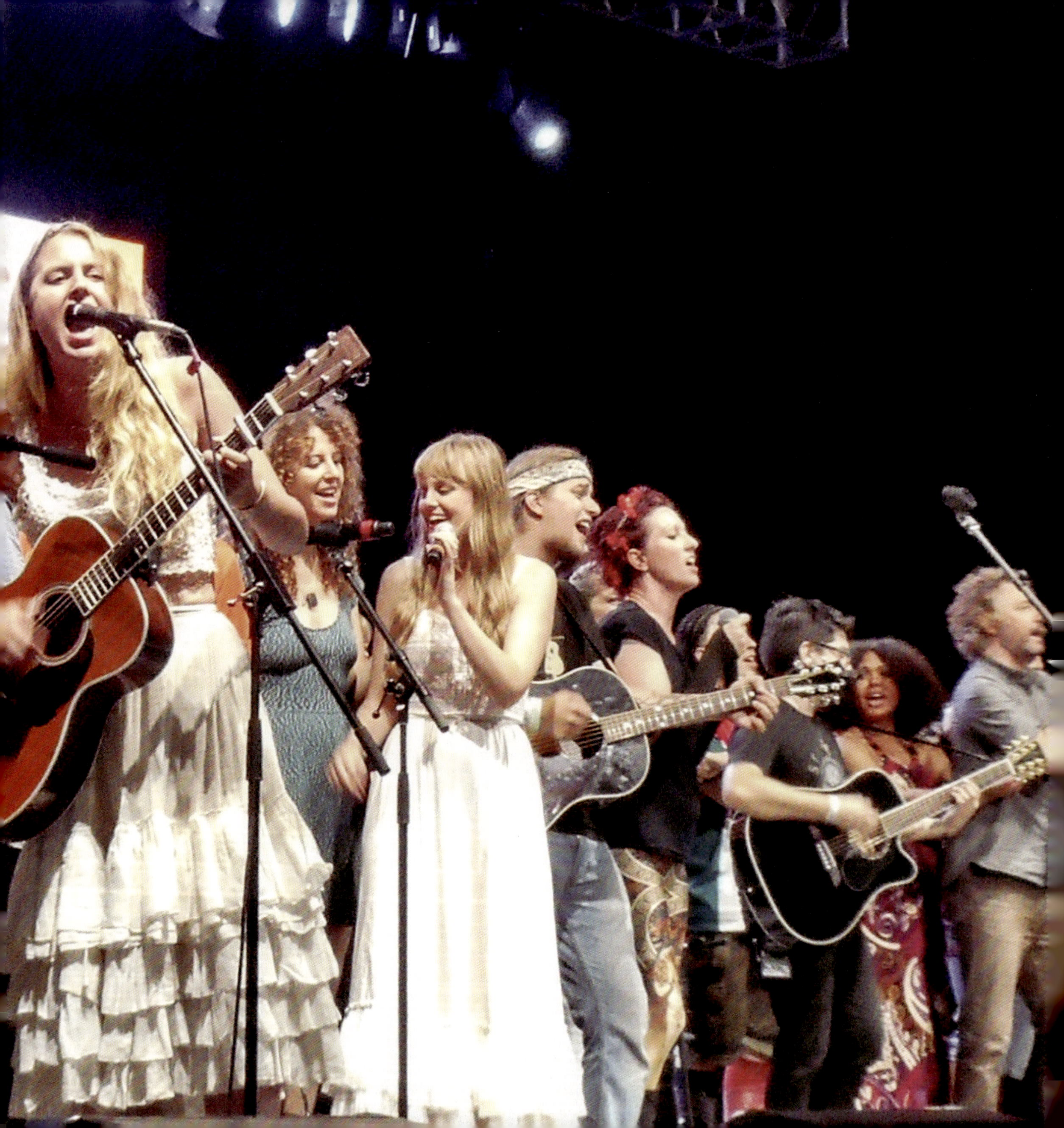

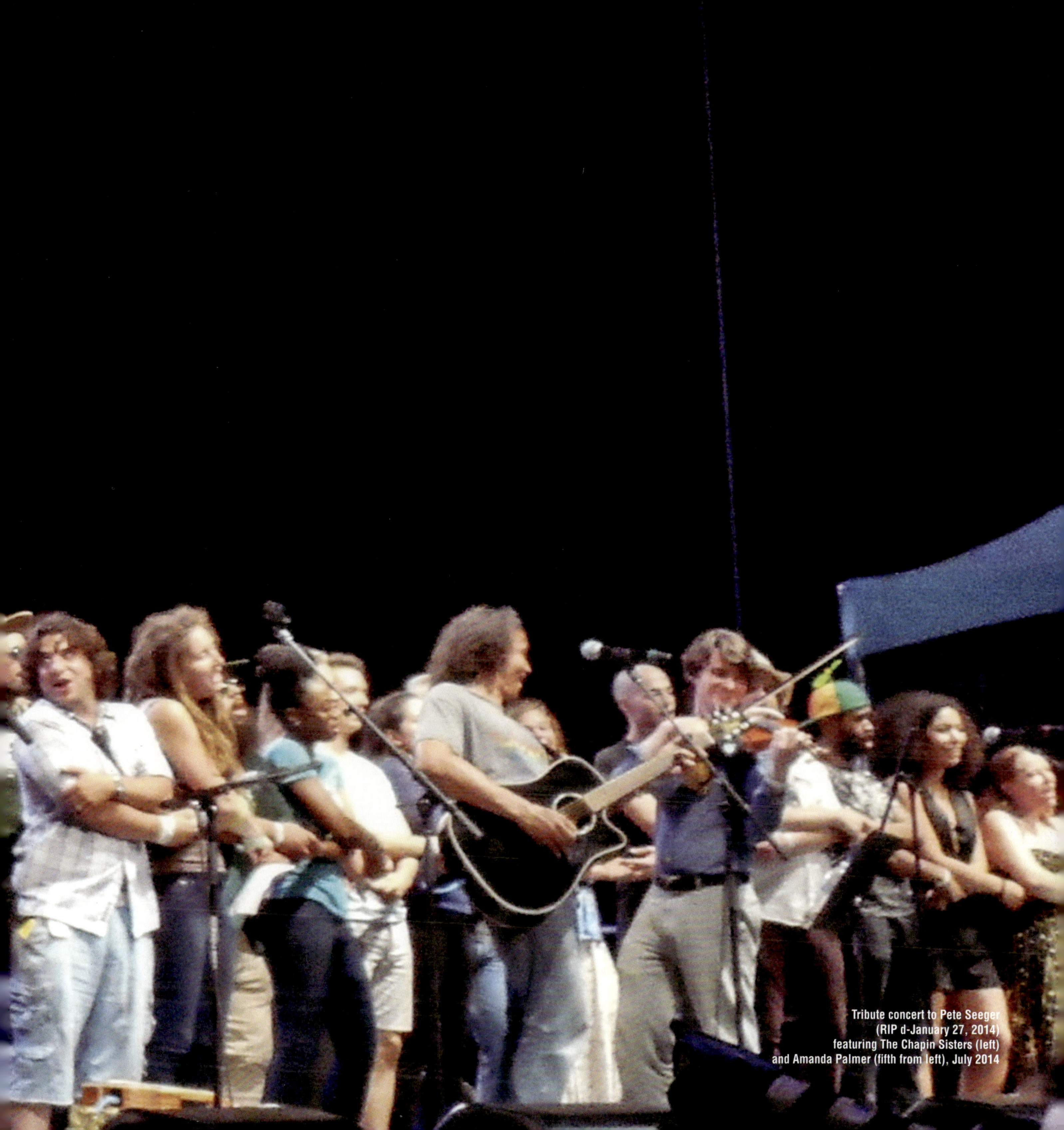

Tribute concert to Pete Seeger
(RIP d-January 27, 2014)
featuring The Chapin Sisters (left)
and Amanda Palmer (fifth from left), July 2014

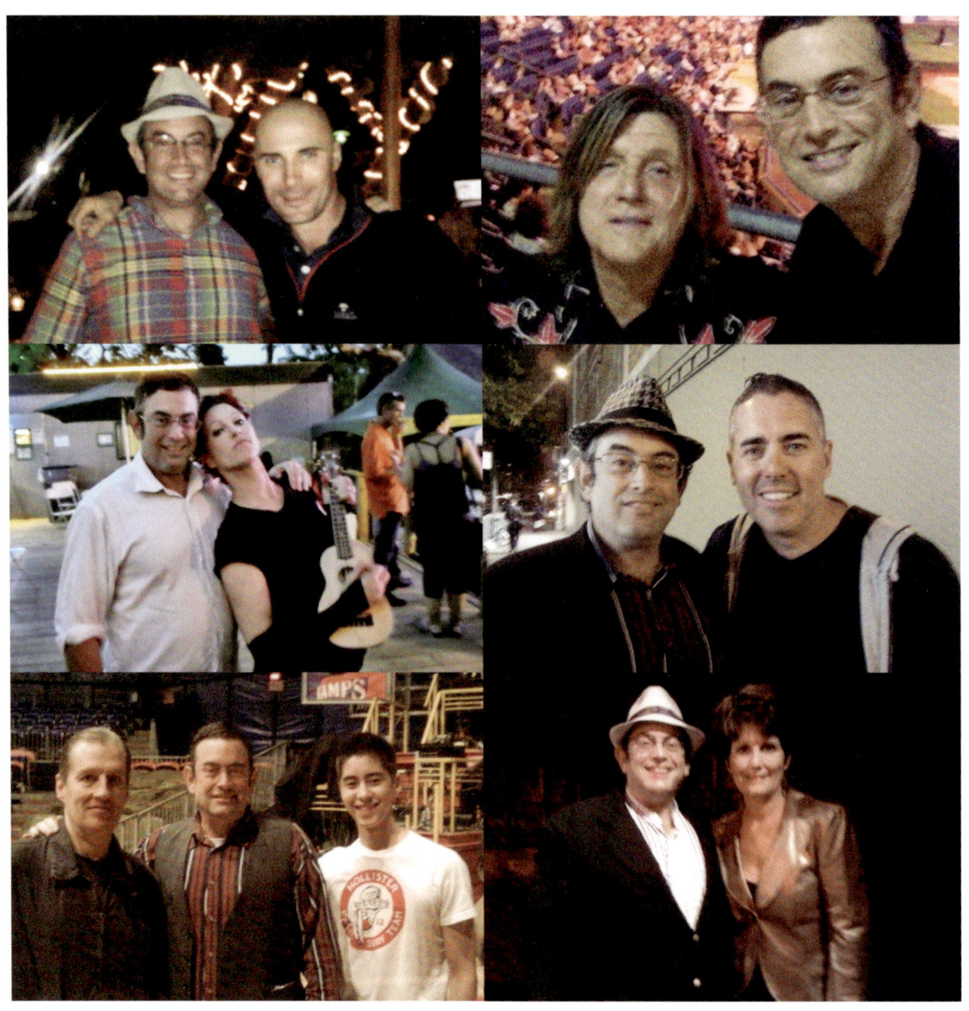

Clockwise from top right:
with Billy J. Kramer
Ed Robertson (Barenaked Ladies)
Lucie Arnaz (singer, actress, daughter of Lucy and Desi)
Ty Tojo and Dick Franco (Big Apple Circus)
Amanda Palmer
Victor Kee (Cirque du Soleil)

# about the author

The author/photographer Roger Harris is also a performing artist and has performed his original stage show, "Sir Juggley's One Man Circus!" over a thousand times. He appears in the Guinness Book of World Records three times. He is the creator of the Jerusalem Circus School for Children, and was proprietor for over ten years. He is a world traveller (over 90 countries), and father of 6. He lives in New York and Miami.

**Books by Roger Harris**

'Crystal Reef'

'Girl With Books' -and other stories

'Religions at War'

'There Once Was a Woman Named Bubbles' - and 200 other limericks

'The Peaceful Home'

'Royal Lunch' -and other stories for children

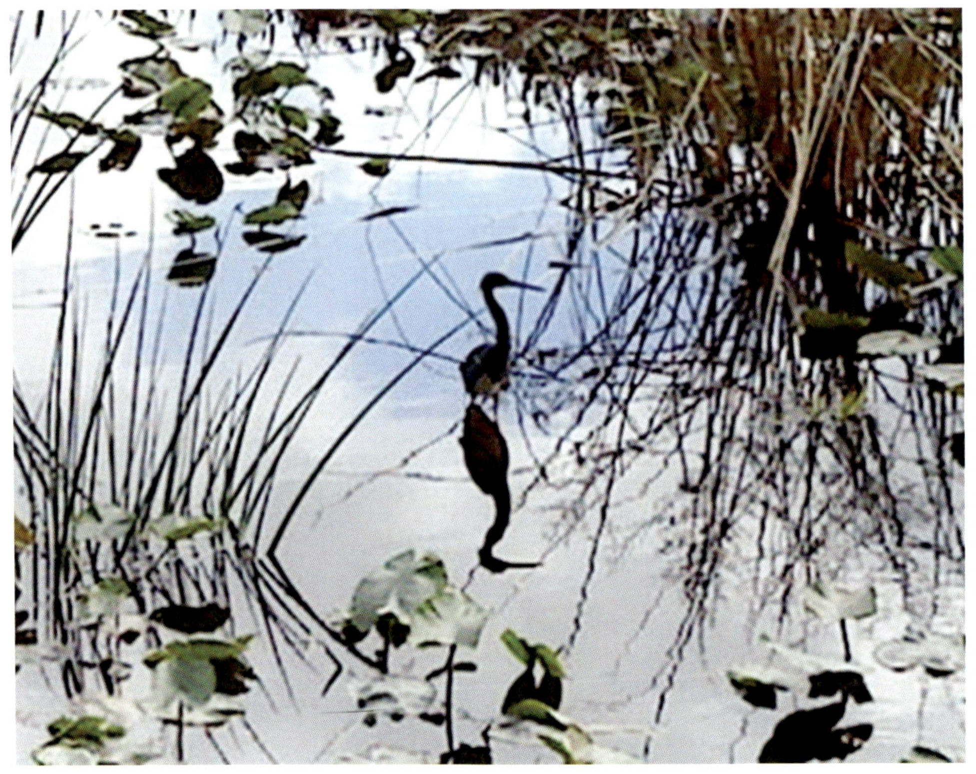

In memory of Irwin Haskell. Beloved father, husband, grandfather.
*by Lloyd, Marla, and Karen Haskell*


In memory of Marcy and Harold Harris.
Beloved parents, grand parents, great grand parents.
*by Lisa, Vicki, Bobby, and Roger Harris*


In memory of Monica Rasch
Beloved mother, grandmother, wife, sister
*by David Rasch*

**Heron, Boynton Beach, Florida**

for Bella
(and all the future rockers)

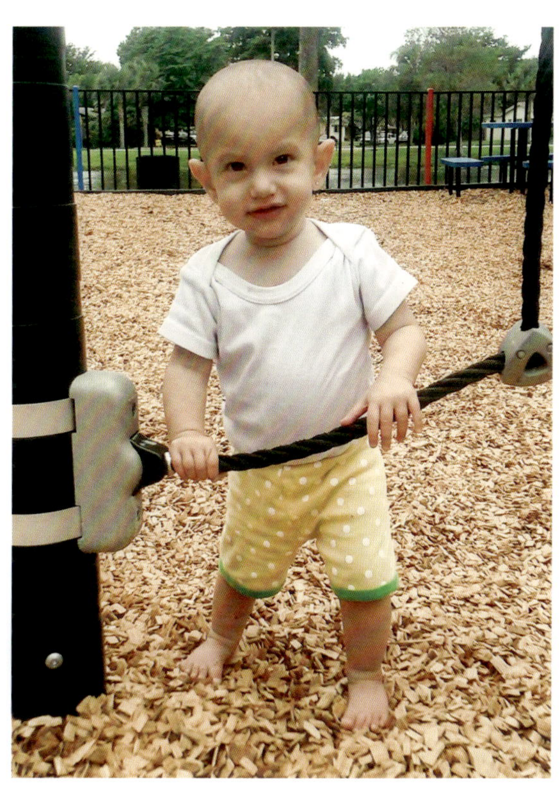

**This Is My Generation**
Rock legends of the 1950s, 60s, 70s, and 80s on stage today

*by Roger Harris*



Published by Damiani
info@damianieditore.com
www.damianieditore.com



Printed in June 2016 by Grafiche Damiani - Faenza Group SpA, Italy

ISBN 9788862084932